Letts
Study Aids

The Mayor of Casterbridge

Thomas Hardy

Guide written and developed by
John Mahoney and Stewart Martin

Charles Letts & Co Ltd
London, Edinburgh & New York

First published 1987
by Charles Letts & Co Ltd
Diary House, Borough Road, London SE1 1DW
Reprinted 1988

Illustration: Peter McClure

The authors gratefully acknowledge the help
given to them by 'The Thomas Hardy Society
Limited' in providing source material for the
map of Casterbridge which appears on p 6.

'Letts' is a registered trademark of
Charles Letts & Co Ltd

Stewart Martin is an Honours graduate of Lancaster University, where he read English
and Sociology. He has worked both in the UK and abroad as a writer, a teacher, and an
educational consultant. He is married with three children, and is currently deputy
headmaster at Ossett School in West Yorkshire.

John Mahoney has taught English for twenty years. He has been head of English
department in three schools and has wide experience of preparing students at all levels
for most examination boards. He has worked both in the UK and North America
producing educational books and computer software on English language and literature.
He is married with three children and lives in Worcestershire.

British Library Cataloguing in Publication Data
  Mahoney, John
  The mayor of Casterbridge: Thomas Hardy: guide –
  (Guides to literature)
  1. Hardy, Thomas, *1840–1928*. Mayor of Casterbridge
  I. Title II. Martin, Stewart III. Series
  823'.8 PR4750.M3

ISBN 0 85097 765 7

Printed and bound in Great Britain by
Charles Letts (Scotland) Ltd

Contents

To the student

This study companion to your English literature text acts as a guide to the novel or play being studied. It suggests ways in which you can explore content and context, and focuses your attention on those matters which will lead to an understanding, appreciative and sensitive response to the work of literature being studied.

Whilst covering all those aspects dealt with in the traditional-style study aid, more importantly, it is a flexible companion to study, enabling you to organize the patterns of study and priorities which reflect your particular needs at any given moment.

Whilst in many places descriptive, it is never prescriptive, always encouraging a sensitive personal response to a work of literature, rather than the shallow repetition of others' opinions. Such objectives have always been those of the good teacher, and have always assisted the student to gain high grades in 16+ examinations in English literature. These same factors are also relevant to students who are doing coursework in English literature for the purposes of continual assessment.

The major part of this guide is the 'Commentary' where you will find a detailed commentary and analysis of all the important things you should know and study for your examination. There is also a section giving practical help on how to study a set text, write the type of essay that will gain high marks, prepare coursework and a guide to sitting examinations.

Used sensibly, this guide will be invaluable in your studies and help ensure your success in the course.

Thomas Hardy

Thomas Hardy was born in 1840 at the village of Bockhampton, not far from Dorchester, the Casterbridge of the novel. He was encouraged to read by his mother, and from his father he learnt to play the violin, acquiring a love of music which is evident in much of his writing. He was educated at the local village school and later at a private school in Dorchester. He received no university training, an omission which was to cause him much intellectual insecurity.

At the age of 16 he was apprenticed to an architect in Dorchester and learnt about the restoration of churches and old houses. In his spare time he undertook the study of the Latin and Greek classics. In 1862 he moved to London to work as an architectural assistant, but in 1867 he returned to Bockhampton because of ill-health. His knowledge of architecture can be seen in the detailed descriptions he gives of the buildings of Casterbridge. In 1870 Hardy visited Cornwall to plan the restoration of a church. During the visit he met Emma Lavinia Gifford whom he married in 1874.

Hardy began writing poems, but abandoned this for prose writing. In 1874 he gave up his career as an architect in order to concentrate on writing. Most of his novels were published in serial form for magazines in England and America. He worried that his writing was suffering because of the need to cater for his serial audience.

After his marriage Hardy moved about a great deal, living in Surbiton, Swanage, Yeovil and Sturminster-Newton. In 1883 he returned to Dorchester to supervise the building of his house into which he moved in 1885. Hardy visited London frequently, meeting other famous literary figures. Many of his novels met with severe criticism and the publication of *Jude the Obscure* in 1896 was given such a hostile reception that Hardy gave up writing novels altogether and went back to poetry.

His marriage to Emma Gifford was not particularly successful, but he stayed with her until she died in 1912. Two years later he married a much younger woman, Florence Dugdale, who had been acting as his secretary. After his death in 1928, his heart was removed and buried in the grave of his first wife at Stinsford near Dorchester.

The Mayor of Casterbridge was written in 1884-85 and first published in serial form in 1886. The main action of the novel occurs in the mid-19th century. The years of Hardy's childhood, and certainly his youthful impressions of people and events in the setting of rural Wessex colour the novel.

Wessex is the name Hardy gives to his fictional county, taken from the name given to the south-west region of England when it was a Saxon kingdom. Casterbridge is based roughly on mid-century Dorchester. All the towns and villages correspond to real places but are given different names so that over the course of several novels Hardy built up an imaginary world.

The 19th century was a time of great change. The growth of industrial towns and the decline in agriculture in the years after the repeal of the Corn Laws transformed a rural way of life that had existed for centuries. Change was not limited to the countryside. Traditional religious beliefs were threatened by new views and the period was one of great doubt. Scientific advances, particularly in the works of Charles Darwin, seemed to challenge the traditional belief that nature was the reflection of God's goodness. The view of nature as a force indifferent to the plight of man and often malevolent towards him is a theme which runs through *The Mayor of Casterbridge*. It was against this background of change, not always desirable to everyone, but nevertheless inevitable, that this novel was written.

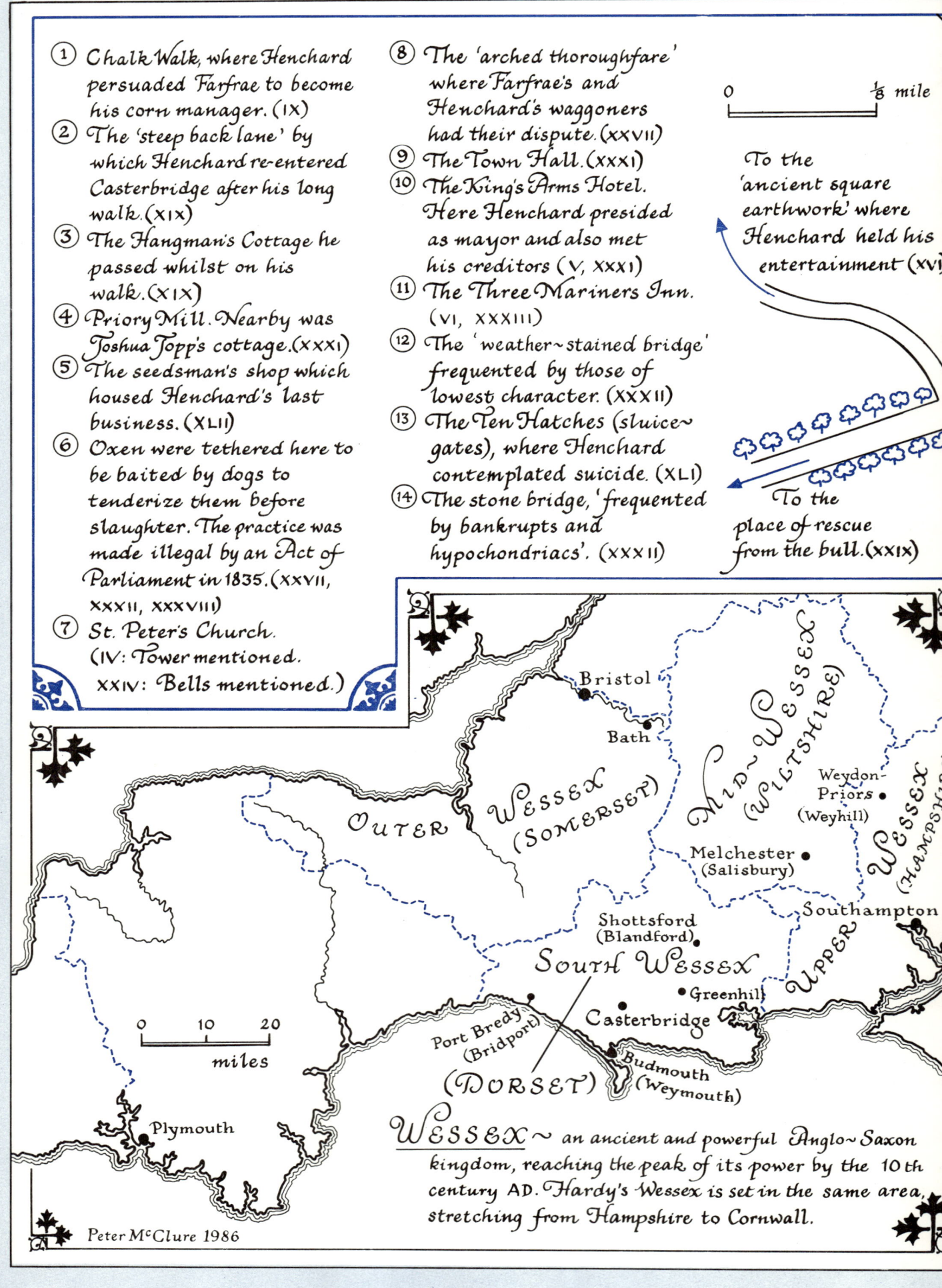

① Chalk Walk, where Henchard persuaded Farfrae to become his corn manager. (IX)

② The 'steep back lane' by which Henchard re-entered Casterbridge after his long walk. (XIX)

③ The Hangman's Cottage he passed whilst on his walk. (XIX)

④ Priory Mill. Nearby was Joshua Jopp's cottage. (XXXI)

⑤ The seedsman's shop which housed Henchard's last business. (XLII)

⑥ Oxen were tethered here to be baited by dogs to tenderize them before slaughter. The practice was made illegal by an Act of Parliament in 1835. (XXVII, XXXII, XXXVIII)

⑦ St. Peter's Church. (IV: Tower mentioned. XXIV: Bells mentioned.)

⑧ The 'arched thoroughfare' where Farfrae's and Henchard's waggoners had their dispute. (XXVII)

⑨ The Town Hall. (XXXI)

⑩ The King's Arms Hotel. Here Henchard presided as mayor and also met his creditors (V, XXXI)

⑪ The Three Mariners Inn. (VI, XXXIII)

⑫ The 'weather-stained bridge' frequented by those of lowest character. (XXXII)

⑬ The Ten Hatches (sluice-gates), where Henchard contemplated suicide. (XLI)

⑭ The stone bridge, 'frequented by bankrupts and hypochondriacs'. (XXXII)

0 ⅛ mile

To the 'ancient square earthwork' where Henchard held his entertainment (XVI)

To the place of rescue from the bull. (XXIX)

Bristol

Bath

OUTER WESSEX (SOMERSET)

MID-WESSEX (WILTSHIRE)

Weydon-Priors (Weyhill)

Melchester (Salisbury)

Southampton

UPPER WESSEX (HAMPSHIRE)

Shottsford (Blandford)

SOUTH WESSEX

Greenhill

Casterbridge

Port Bredy (Bridport)

Budmouth (Weymouth)

(DORSET)

0 10 20 miles

Plymouth

WESSEX ~ an ancient and powerful Anglo-Saxon kingdom, reaching the peak of its power by the 10th century AD. Hardy's Wessex is set in the same area, stretching from Hampshire to Cornwall.

Peter McClure 1986

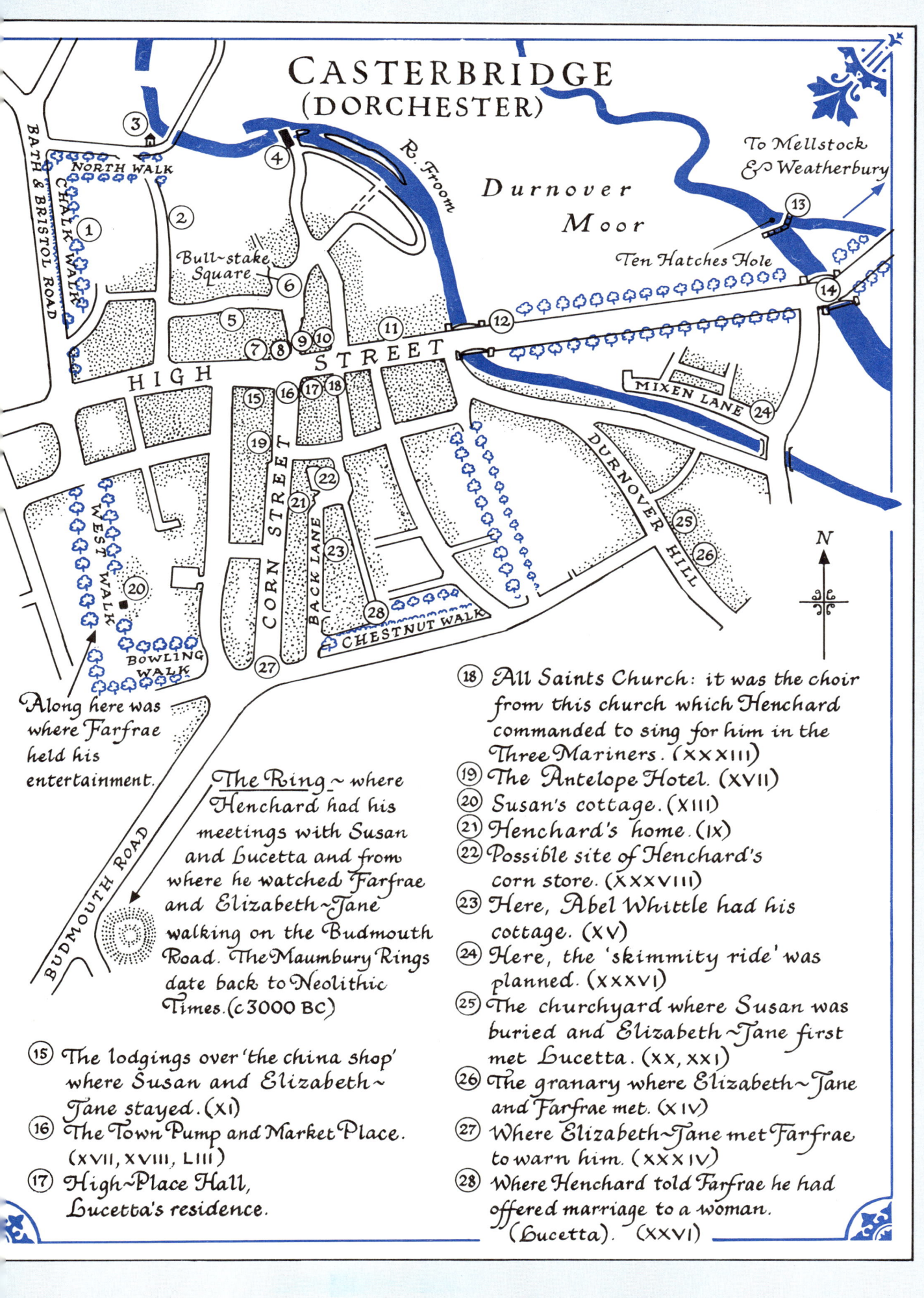

CASTERBRIDGE
(DORCHESTER)

R. Froom

To Mellstock & Weatherbury

Durnover Moor

Ten Hatches Hole

NORTH WALK

BATH & BRISTOL ROAD

CHALK WALK

Bull-stake Square

HIGH STREET

MIXEN LANE

DURNOVER HILL

N

WEST WALK

CORN STREET

BACK LANE

CHESTNUT WALK

BOWLING WALK

Along here was where Farfrae held his entertainment.

BUDMOUTH ROAD

The Ring ~ where Henchard had his meetings with Susan and Lucetta and from where he watched Farfrae and Elizabeth~Jane walking on the Budmouth Road. The Maumbury Rings date back to Neolithic Times. (c 3000 BC)

(15) The lodgings over 'the china shop' where Susan and Elizabeth~ Jane stayed. (XI)

(16) The Town Pump and Market Place. (XVII, XVIII, LIII)

(17) High~Place Hall, Lucetta's residence.

(18) All Saints Church: it was the choir from this church which Henchard commanded to sing for him in the Three Mariners. (XXXIII)

(19) The Antelope Hotel. (XVII)

(20) Susan's cottage. (XIII)

(21) Henchard's home. (IX)

(22) Possible site of Henchard's corn store. (XXXVIII)

(23) Here, Abel Whittle had his cottage. (XV)

(24) Here, the 'skimmity ride' was planned. (XXXVI)

(25) The churchyard where Susan was buried and Elizabeth~Jane first met Lucetta. (XX, XXI)

(26) The granary where Elizabeth~Jane and Farfrae met. (XIV)

(27) Where Elizabeth~Jane met Farfrae to warn him. (XXXIV)

(28) Where Henchard told Farfrae he had offered marriage to a woman. (Lucetta). (XXVI)

Understanding The Mayor of Casterbridge

An exploration of the major topics and themes in the novel

Summaries of themes

Setting

Through the pages of *The Mayor of Casterbridge* we see reflected the intimate knowledge and interest that Hardy had in the changing face of rural England. That knowledge is reflected in the fascinating and detailed accounts of local architecture, references to customs, dialect, economic and social pressures, and history.

In many lyrical passages he makes evocative use of natural, historic and urban settings, of which you will do well to take note, for they form an important part of the intricate web of plot and characterization that he weaves for his reader. Note, for example, how the historic setting and description of the Ring evokes the gloomiest and most threatening of atmospheres. Whether it be the countryside or the urban setting of Casterbridge, the detailed descriptions bring both place and people alive.

Those aspects which are mentioned below deal briefly with the very many facets of this novel's setting.

Agriculture Casterbridge is portrayed as a town whose existence depends on agriculture and it completes the picture of rural life about which Hardy is writing. There are no suburbs and the class of objects in the shops confirms that agriculture pervades business activity. In the centre of the town is a busy market place where produce and labour are bought and sold.

During the 19th century far-reaching changes were occurring in agricultural methods and this too is evident in the novel. In chapter 1 the turnip-hoer mentions that houses are being pulled down in Weydon-Priors, and chapter 24 relates the arrival of the horse drill to Casterbridge. In later years agriculture was to decline severely, but in the Casterbridge of the mid-19th century it affected the lives of farmers, professional people and townsfolk alike.

Corn trade The novel is based in the years of the uncertain harvests which immediately preceded the repeal of the Corn Laws. The corn trade is the most important aspect of agricultural life in Casterbridge. The Corn Laws were introduced in 1815 at the end of the Napoleonic Wars, when the import of foreign grain became possible again. The increase in competition caused a surplus of grain and prices fell, threatening many farmers with bankruptcy – the fate that eventually befell Henchard. The 1815 parliament fixed a price of 80 shillings a quarter, and if prices fell below this, imports were stopped. In 1828 a sliding scale was introduced, but the general effect of these measures was to give home-dealers considerable control over prices enabling corn-merchants rapidly to grow rich.

Architecture Thomas Hardy trained and worked as an architect before concentrating on writing. Consequently, there are many detailed descriptions of the architectural features of Casterbridge buildings. The description of the Three Mariners inn in chapter 6 paints a colourful picture of this ancient inn – unfortunately now demolished. High-Place Hall is also described in similar detail in chapter 21. Note however, that these descriptions are not just unrelated additions to the story. They give a reality and presence to the events taking place within their confines, so that we see the places as real and the lives of the people who inhabit them equally real.

Change Change is a theme which persists throughout the novel. Historical settings help to locate the story in time and show that change is an inevitable, unending process.

Changes were occurring in agricultural life with the introduction of new methods and machinery. Farfrae represents the new approach, replacing verbal agreements and 'rules of thumb' with letters and ledgers. Although change is often for the better, the 'rugged picturesqueness' of the old methods disappears as well. Modes of transport were changing with much of the trade of waggoners being taken by the new railways.

The 19th century was also a time of great social change. The great Victorian ideal of self-help and an adventurous business spirit was much to the fore; certainly Farfrae is an example of this, and so to an extent is Elizabeth-Jane with her great thirst for respectability and improving herself through reading.

Clothes Descriptions of the clothing of the characters serve to outline their personalities, occupations and social position. At the beginning of the novel there is a detailed description of the hay-trusser's manner of dress in chapter 1, and later of Henchard as a successful civic dignitary in chapter 5. The characters of Elizabeth-Jane and Lucetta are seen in contrast and this is most obvious in the way they dress. Elizabeth-Jane dresses modestly even when her circumstances suddenly improve. Lucetta is far more showy, and the cherry coloured dress she chooses suggests that her moral standards may not be in keeping with strict Victorian principles. After his bankruptcy, Henchard continues to wear his genteel clothes, showing that he is a man who has seen better times, before reverting completely to the clothes worn by a hay-trusser.

Marriage The way that marriage is criticized in the novel seems to reflect Hardy's own disillusionment with the legal and moral obligations it entailed. In the first chapter he comments that nothing but marriage could have accounted for the atmosphere of stale familiarity between the couple as they walked along the road to Weydon-Priors.

The marriage of Susan and Henchard gives her nothing but temper from Henchard and stifles his ambitions. For the male characters in the novel, marriage is more often a dutiful and socially convenient arrangement. Despite her changeable nature, Lucetta expresses her love and devotion to Farfrae, whereas Elizabeth-Jane's marriage to Farfrae enables her to live a reasonably comfortable life in the knowledge that Farfrae will not make any great emotional demands on her. You might like to consider in some detail what the three male characters, Farfrae, Henchard and Newson, expected from marriage, and compare their expectations with those of Lucetta, Susan and Elizabeth-Jane.

Money As stated previously the 19th century was a time of great rural change. Small farmers who produced enough to eat well being replaced by bigger farmers and the intermediary of the corn-factor who profited from dealing in grain. Money and banks become crucial to the new type of business arrangements, as we see when Henchard's speculations start to go wrong. The bank provides the funds for his dealings and when he fails they take possession of his business. The importance of money as a criterion for success applies equally to wage earners who 'know nothing, sir, outside of eight shillings a week', and to ladies setting up house in style on the strength of an inheritance.

Propriety The moral standards of the Victorians were quite different to the standards of today. Elizabeth-Jane's sense of moral outrage at Lucetta's marriage to Farfrae when she is promised to Henchard might seem a bit strange to us, but it was contrary to the Victorian sense of propriety. Elizabeth-Jane's insistence on correctness makes her reject Henchard when he most needs her. It is not until it is too late that she realizes her unkindness.

Superstition

Hardy showed great interest in the superstitions and folklore of the old rural life. Henchard's visit to the weather prophet shows that he is ashamed to admit his belief in such superstitious nonsense, but, not being a man of science, he needs to find a reason for his actions. It is obvious that many other farmers feel the same way from the fact that the weather prophet makes a comfortable living.

Henchard is a superstitious person and although he cannot admit that Farfrae is roasting a waxen image of him, he often feels that some sinister force is working against him.

Structure

Throughout the story, the thoughtful reader will find many 'clues' to what is happening – for example, the matter of the colour of Elizabeth-Jane's eyes gives us an indication that all is not as it should be, if she is supposed to be Henchard's daughter. There is the instance of the stranger 'walking the plank' into Casterbridge: is this an implied reference to his origins and therefore his identity? Note how the furmity woman always seems to appear at crucial moments in Henchard's life.

There is a clear association with the movement of the seasons with many events taking place after harvest in the autumn. There are events that parallel and contrast one another: the two scenes where Henchard and Farfrae each hold sway at different times in the Three Mariners; the two 'rides' that all the town turn out to see – the skimmington ride, and the royal visit – and which bode ill for Lucetta and Henchard; the fight between the two carters which foreshadows that of Henchard and Farfrae, the five guineas that Henchard gets for Susan, and later returns to her. Do be aware of how these events all dovetail one into the other. Some of them are dealt with in more detail in the commentary.

It is also worth noting that the novel can be divided into four sections each shorter than the previous one. These are: chapters 1–31, 32–40, 41–43 and 44–45. The movement of each section is the same. Each has an initial situation which seems to offer some hope for Henchard, followed by events which create doubt, fear and anxious anticipation for an outcome that results, finally, as a catastrophe.

Letters   There are many occasions when letters and notes appear in the novel. They are a narrative device to help the plot along and may make an immediate impact or introduce mystery and suspense into the story. Lucetta is frequently writing notes and letters. It is her reference to past letters to Henchard which creates the most suspense and has far-reaching consequences. You might like to consider whether occasionally the plot relies a little too heavily on the coincidence of badly-sealed letters and packages.

Contrast   There are many contrasts of character and events in the novel which pattern and balance the structure of the book. Henchard and Farfrae are contrasting personalities, as are Lucetta and Elizabeth-Jane. Farfrae's success is seen as a contrast to Henchard's failure. The rustics contrast tragedy with humour in their comments. An example of this is the conversations round the town pump after the death of Susan in chapter 18.

Suspense   *The Mayor of Casterbridge*, like many of Hardy's novels, was first published in serial form. Many of the chapters end on a note of suspense as, for example, when Lucetta hides behind a curtain expecting Henchard to be the visitor. Suspense creates tension in the novel which propels the story along. Letters are used as a device to create suspense, and the appearance of a stranger in Casterbridge who shows no surprise at the unusual way of getting to Mixen Lane, excites our interest in his identity.

To appreciate the multitude of incidents and their associations you must read carefully and thoughtfully. If you do not, then you lose much of the enjoyment to be gained from a well-constructed story.

Nature

The countryside and towns of rural England are not a mere backcloth to the workings of the plot but an integral part of its conception. Consider also how the antics of human nature are central to the novel.

Note how Hardy uses the image of caged and free birds to reflect aspects of characters' lives, their moods, and the atmosphere around them. You should look for examples of how the natural world is used to create mood and tension in the story.

Be aware of the conflict with nature which seems to be part of Henchard's life and its seeming perverseness in relation to his fortunes. It is a problem with his wheat that brings Farfrae into his life, and a misreading of the harvest prospects that lead to Farfrae taking over completely.

The weather acts in two significant ways in the novel. Firstly, it is of great importance in determining the success or failure of the harvest, upon which the wealth of the community depends. A bad harvest could double the price of corn in a few weeks. The weather is held in awe, as though it were a god.

Secondly, the weather is used to form a sympathetic background or create a mood against which the action occurs. The wedding day of Henchard and Susan is one on which there is warm November rain, suggesting a dutiful rather than joyous occasion.

Aspects of character

This book is largely a study of one man and the troubles he faces. You should look to see what are the driving forces behind his actions and attitudes. How does he respond to events and people? Does he change in any way as the story unfolds? Does he learn by his and other's mistakes? What are the strong and weak points of character that go to make up the man? You should consider these questions, the points below, and the very many other human emotions and character traits which influence actions – both in relation to Henchard and the other characters in the story.

Ambition Ambition is the driving force behind several characters in the novel. It is ambition which makes Henchard restless as a young man and enables him to build up a successful corn-trading business in Casterbridge. Farfrae is also an ambitious young man who has left his country in order to seek his fortune. He substitutes ambition for love when he decides not to propose to Elizabeth-Jane.

Susan Newson is also ambitious, but in a different way. Her ambitions are realized when she marries Henchard and finds promise of a better life for Elizabeth-Jane.

Defiance Henchard is physically a very powerful man and his attitude to life reflects this power. He often feels that a sinister force is working against him and reacts to the indifference of fate with a grim defiance. This is in contrast to Elizabeth-Jane, for instance, who accepts the unforeseen quietly and calmly.

Impulse and calculation Impulsiveness is a feature of Henchard's character. His sale of Susan, his treatment of Abel Whittle and his dismissal of Farfrae are all examples of his impulsive nature. In contrast, Farfrae is a much more calculating person and even when he attributes Henchard's generous offer of the post of manager to providence, he has obviously thought long and hard about the consequences of accepting it.

Kindness Elizabeth-Jane possesses a natural kindness. Despite Henchard's attitude towards her when he discovers that she is not his daughter, she continues to care for him, looks after him in illness and eventually goes to live with him when she realizes how desperate he is.

Although Farfrae is kind and generous to Henchard after his bankruptcy, his kindness is often tempered by his calculating nature.

Love The shame and guilt which Henchard feels after he has sold his wife make him substitute ambition for love. He becomes a successful man, but is very lonely. His first attempt to realize his need to love is his relationship with Farfrae which ends disastrously. Likewise, his relationship with Elizabeth-Jane turns sour when he realizes she is not his daughter. All his attempts to love are thwarted by his pride and jealousy. Towards the end of the novel he learns to love Elizabeth-Jane for what she is, and when he returns to Casterbridge on her wedding day, he thinks only of her happiness. Ironically, his love is rejected and he goes away to die alone, although eventually his repentance wins the love of Elizabeth-Jane.

Pride Henchard's strong sense of pride is illustrated when Nance Mockridge reveals that Elizabeth-Jane once waited on customers at the Three Mariners inn in chapter 20. Another example is his reaction when Farfrae opposes his humiliation of Abel Whittle. His pride is damaged by the fact that Farfrae opposes him in front of his men.

Although Susan is seen as a weak person by Henchard, the blow to her pride when he auctions her is evident in the anger with which she hurls her wedding ring at him.

Shallowness   Despite Farfrae's ability to express great emotion in the songs of his native country, there is no real depth to his feelings. As Hardy comments when he describes Farfrae's singing at his wedding to Elizabeth-Jane, he gives strong expression to a song of his native country that he loves so well as never to have revisited it. Farfrae is incapable of understanding the deep emotions which rule Henchard. His relationships with women also show a shallowness of emotion.

Shame   Guilt and shame are feelings which rule Henchard. The guilt he feels after selling his wife and daughter is tempered by the sense of shame he has for his actions. His vow to avoid strong liquor is an attempt to overcome his shame by proving the strength of his will.

Temper   Henchard's temper is evident from the comments of his wife before she leaves him. It is still present, albeit under the surface, when she sees him through the window of the King's Arms nineteen years later. His bad temper often makes him behave violently, as when he forces the choir to sing Psalm 109. He cools as quickly as he flares, and excuses his behaviour by saying he is a fearful practical joker.

Deception

It could be argued that deceit is one of the major forces which change the lives of the main characters. It is the spring for most of the action that occurs in the story. It starts from the moment that Henchard deceives himself that he is making a real effort to trace his wife and child. It continues with Susan deceiving Henchard that Elizabeth-Jane is his daughter. Henchard does not tell Farfrae the whole story of his life, as indeed Lucetta holds things back from Elizabeth-Jane. Lucetta lives in fear of Farfrae finding out about her past. Elizabeth-Jane is deceived by Henchard, Susan and Lucetta.

These qualities are evident in the contrasting characters of Lucetta and Elizabeth-Jane. The artful Lucetta uses lies and deceptions to manipulate people for her own ends. It shows in the different ways in which Henchard and Farfrae conduct their lives. Deception is a thread woven throughout the entire novel.

Are Farfrae and Elizabeth-Jane the most honest and straightforward characters in the novel? Or does the taint of deception touch even them in some ways?

Loneliness

Note how Lucetta and Henchard seem driven by impulse to confide in complete strangers. Is it that loneliness drives them to it? They seem unable to make satisfactory relationships with other people. Think about the faults in their characters that lead to this state of affairs.

Consider Elizabeth-Jane. Remember how we first meet her, hand in hand with Susan on the road to Weydon-Priors. With her mother's death and Henchard's sudden, strange rejection of her what must she have felt? Was she a very lonely character?

Is Farfrae lonely? Does he not need people in the same way that Henchard does? It could be that he is a very shallow character or, conversely, just independent. Consider the similarities of character between him and Newson in this respect.

As well as considering the above points you should also note the recurring image of travellers on a lonely road. Despite the fact that the story centres on the town of Casterbridge, there is a great deal which relates to the loneliness of the open road. Note also how the pastoral setting in which these travellers find themselves often echoes their loneliness.

Irony

Irony illustrates the intervention of fate in the action, when the result or consequence of an action is not what is expected. There are many incidents in the novel where the irony of the situation points to the very perversity of fate. The atmosphere of tragedy which pervades the novel is rooted in the consequences of the main characters' words and actions, many of which are tinged with irony. Lucetta vows not to be a 'slave to the past' but becomes one. Newson 'pays' for the death of Lucetta by contributing money for the skimmington ride. There are many such instances, particularly in relation to Henchard. Your attention will be drawn to them in the commentary.

Fate

Is Man responsible for his actions and does he ignore his past deeds at his peril? Or even if he tries to learn from his past deeds can he still control his future? To some extent the flaws in Henchard's character are the cause of his downfall, and fate decrees that his character will not enable him to overcome those flaws. Certainly, at times Henchard seems to have the feeling that he is fighting an unequal battle against the perverse nature of an unpredictable and uncontrollable fate.

Henchard has to learn to accept responsibility for events which are beyond his control. His mistaken business transactions are largely responsible for his bankruptcy, but the motive of revenge against Farfrae which leads him to make those transactions is the source of his disastrous failure in business.

The story of *The Mayor of Casterbridge* follows the rise and fall of the tragic hero Michael Henchard. His fall is due largely to his inability to come to terms with his past. The tragedy of Henchard's fall is made all the more real because, although he is capable of great cruelty, fate often intervenes to snatch away what little happiness he has. We come to pity him, because, despite his tremendous efforts to determine his destiny, he is unable to avoid defeat.

Rustics

As in Greek tragedy, the rustics form a chorus which comments on the action and provides background information. The rustics differ from the chorus in that Hardy uses them as individual voices. They provide a contrast to the more middle-class business community and complete our view of Casterbridge society. One of their main functions is to introduce humour into the story, which is often contrasted by a more pathetic comment. An example of this is when Christopher Coney digs up the four pence used to close Susan's eyes after her death, and spends them at the Three Mariners.

Finding your way around the commentary

Each page of the commentary gives the following information:

1   A quotation from the start of each paragraph on which a comment is made, or act/scene or line numbers plus a quotation, so that you can easily locate the right place in your text.

2   A series of comments, explaining, interpreting, and drawing your attention to important incidents, characters and aspects of the text.

3   For each comment, headings to indicate the important characters, themes, and ideas dealt with in the comment.

4   For each heading, a note of the comment numbers in this guide where the previous or next comment dealing with that heading occurred.

Thus you can use this commentary section in a number of ways.

1   Turn to that part of the commentary dealing with the chapter/act you are perhaps revising for a class discussion or essay. Read through the comments in sequence, referring all the time to the text, which you should have open before you. The comments will direct your attention to all the important things of which you should take note.

2   Take a single character or topic from the list on page 15. Note the comment number next to it. Turn to that comment in this guide, where you will find the first of a number of comments on your chosen topic. Study it, and the appropriate part of your text to which it will direct you. Note the comment number in this guide where the next comment for your topic occurs and turn to it when you are ready. Thus, you can follow one topic right through your text. If you have an essay to write on a particular character or theme just follow the path through this guide and you will soon find everything you need to know!

3   A number of relevant relationships between characters and topics are listed on page 15. To follow these relationships throughout your text, turn to the comment indicated. As the previous and next comment are printed at the side of each page in the commentary, it is a simple matter to flick through the pages to find the previous or next occurrence of the relationship in which you are interested.

For example, you want to examine in depth the theme of loneliness in the novel. Turning to the single topic list, you will find that this theme first occurs in comment 16. On turning to comment 16 you will discover a zero (0) in the place of the previous reference (because this is the first time that it has occurred) and the number 25 for the next reference. You now turn to comment 25 and find that the previous comment number is 16 (from where you have just been looking) and that the next reference is to comment 26, and so on throughout the text.

You also wish to trace the relationship between Henchard and Farfrae throughout the novel. From the relationships list, you are directed to comment 49. This is the first time that both Henchard and Farfrae are discussed together and you will find that the next time that this happens occurs in comment 50 (the 'next' reference for both Henchard and Farfrae). On to comment 50 and the next number is 51; you will now discover that two different comment numbers are given for the subject under examination – numbers 54 and 56. This is because each character is traced separately as well as together and you will have to continue tracing them separately until you finally come to comment 59 – the next occasion on which both Henchard and Farfrae are discussed.

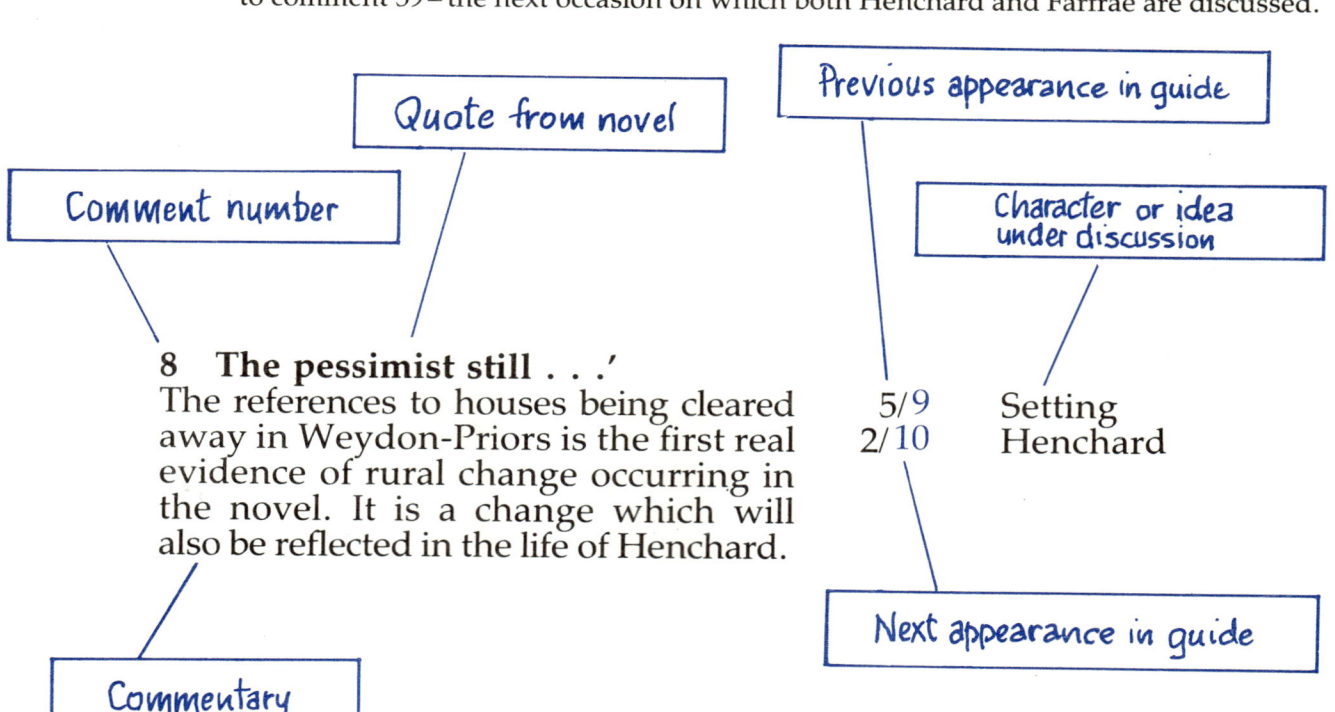

Quote from novel

Previous appearance in guide

Comment number

Character or idea under discussion

8   The pessimist still . . .'
The references to houses being cleared away in Weydon-Priors is the first real evidence of rural change occurring in the novel. It is a change which will also be reflected in the life of Henchard.

5/9   Setting
2/10   Henchard

Next appearance in guide

Commentary

Single topics:

	Comment no:		Comment no:
Henchard	2	Setting	1
Farfrae	49	Structure	3
		Nature	1
Susan	4	Character	10
Elizabeth-Jane	25		
Lucetta	152	Deception	20
		Loneliness	16
Newson	13	Irony	31
Joshua Jopp	85	Fate	1
Abel Whittle	133	Rustics	45

Relationships:

			Comment no:
Henchard	and	Susan	12
Henchard	and	Elizabeth-Jane	46
Henchard	and	Lucetta	155
Henchard	and	Farfrae	49
Henchard	and	Newson	63
Henchard	and	Joshua Jopp	86
Henchard	and	Character	10
Henchard	and	Deception	20
Henchard	and	Loneliness	16
Henchard	and	Character	9
Farfrae	and	Elizabeth-Jane	50
Farfrae	and	Character	49
Lucetta	and	Elizabeth-Jane	179
Lucetta	and	Farfrae	202
Lucetta	and	Deception	155
Lucetta	and	Character	188
Susan	and	Elizabeth-Jane	25
Susan	and	Deception	20
Susan	and	Character	16

Analysis chart

Dates and time sequences — The story starts 'before the nineteenth century had reached one-third of its span'	1	2	3	4	5	6	7	8	9	10	11	12	13	14	15	16	17	18	19
	Late summer	16 September	18 years later	One evening in mid-September					Next day		That evening	Later that evening	Mid-November						Three weeks after Susan's funeral
Chapter	1	2	3	4	5	6	7	8	9	10	11	12	13	14	15	16	17	18	19

Important events

Chapter	1	2	3	4	5	6	7	8	9	10	11	12	13	14	15	16	17	18	19
Event	Auction of Susan	Henchard's vow	Susan and Elizabeth-Jane reappear	Susan and Elizabeth-Jane arrive at Casterbridge	Henchard discovered as Mayor of Casterbridge		Farfrae and Henchard meet	Farfrae sings in Three Mariners inn	Farfrae made corn manager	Henchard and Elizabeth-Jane meet	Susan and Henchard meet	Henchard tells Farfrae of his past	Susan and Henchard married		Dispute over Abel Whittle	Farfrae dismissed by Henchard		Susan dies. Lucetta writes to Henchard	Henchard reads Susan's letter

Places	1	2	3	4	5	6	7	8	9	10	11	12	13	14	15	16	17	18	19
Casterbridge		•		●————————————————————→								●————————————————————————————————→							
Weydon-Priors	•		•																
Ring at Budmouth											•								

Characters	1	2	3	4	5	6	7	8	9	10	11	12	13	14	15	16	17	18	19
Henchard	•	•	•	•	•	•	•	•	•	•	•	•	•	•	•	•	•	•	•
Farfrae							•	•	•	•		•		•	•	•	•		
Susan	•	•	•	•	•	•	•	•	•		•		•	•				•	
Elizabeth-Jane			•	•		•	•	•	•	•				•	•	•	•		•
Lucetta																		•	
Newson	•			•			•												
Joshua Jopp										•									
Abel Whittle															•				

Aspects	1	2	3	4	5	6	7	8	9	10	11	12	13	14	15	16	17	18	19
Setting	•	•	•	•	•	•	•	•	•	•	•	•	•	•				•	•
Structure	•	•			•	•	•		•	•	•	•		•			•	•	•
Nature	•				•		•						•			•			
Character	•	•			•	•	•	•		•		•	•	•	•	•	•	•	•
Deception		•	•	•			•	•			•	•	•		•			•	
Loneliness	•		•					•				•						•	•
Irony			•		•		•	•	•	•		•	•					•	•
Fate	•	•	•			•			•			•		•			•	•	•
Rustics					•			•					•					•	

	1	2	3	4	5	6	7	8	9	10	11	12	13	14	15	16	17	18	19
Page in commentary on which chapter first appears	19	21	22	23	25	26	26	28	28	30	31	33	34	35	36	37	38	39	40

	20	21	22	23	24	25	26	27	28	29	30	31	32	33	34	35	36	37	38	39	40	41	42	43	44	45
Date	16 October		2 February				Spring – August	September				September: 21 years after auction													11 November	December
Event	Lucetta arrives		Lucetta and Farfrae meet		Lucetta confides in Elizabeth-Jane		Henchard engages Joshua Jopp		Furmity woman tells of the auction	Henchard discovers Lucetta and Farfrae are married	Henchard bankrupt: moves in with Jopp	Henchard released from his vow		Henchard reads Lucetta's letters to Farfrae		Skimmington ride planned	Royal visitor	Farfrae and Henchard fight	Skimmington ride	Lucetta dies	Newson comes — and goes		Newson returns. Henchard leaves Casterbridge		Elizabeth-Jane and Farfrae married	Henchard dies
Page	41	43	43	44	46	46	47	49	50	51	51	52	53	54	55	55	56	57	57	58	58	59	60	61	62	63

Commentary

Chapter 1

1 One evening of late . . .
The opening paragraph of the story presents us with the 'large village of Weydon-Priors' and a young couple covered in dust which lent a 'disadvantageous shabbiness' to their appearance. Both the village and the couple will undergo startling changes in the immediate and long-term future. The 'disadvantage' which nature's dust has laid on the couple hints at how the whims of nature and Fate will affect the pair in the future.

0/13	Fate
0/4	Nature
0/2	Setting

2 The man was . . .
Henchard is introduced to us a fine figure; not a labourer, but a skilled countryman carrying the tools of his trade. Note, however, the 'dogged and cynical [personal] indifference' he displays – hinting at the misfortune which will beset him in the course of the story.

1/5	Setting
0/8	Henchard

3 What was really . . .
The silence of the couple, the lack of physical contact and the comment that she appeared to receive his 'ignoring silence' as a natural thing, partly prepare us for the shock of the auction scene about to be enacted.

0/5	Structure

4 The chief – almost . . .
Some hint of how nature mirrors and to an extent controls the destinies of the characters is seen here. The contrast apparent between the 'handsome' girl with 'fire on her lips' and the girl with 'the hard, half-apathetic expression' could not be more startling. Yet note how it is the influence of nature's light and shade which causes such a dramatic difference in our perception of her.

0/5	Nature
0/12	Susan

5 The chief – almost . . .
'Time and chance . . . the work of Nature . . . [and] civilization' provides a summary of the major themes of the novel. The passage of time will lead to great changes, but like nature, some things will go full circle: think of Henchard's fortunes at the the beginning and end of the novel. Nature provides a backdrop and at the same time a pervasive influence on the lives of all characters. Civilization, the movement of past into present, from prehistoric works through Roman influence to present day are all reflected in this novel. They all have a part to play in speaking of the passage of man through time, and the trials and tribulations which beset him on his passage.

4/6	Nature
2/8	Setting
3/7	Structure

6 The wife mostly . . .
Do not skip over these lyrical passages which present the natural scene. They add an emotion and rhythm to the story, supporting the narrative and reflecting the almost relentless movement of the characters towards their individual destinies.

5/7	Nature

7 For a long time . . .
The image of the bird, caged and free, appears a number of times. It reflects some of the emotions and trials of various characters. Note how the 'weak bird' and its 'trite old evening song' echo the feeling we get about the tired relationship between the man and woman, and the 'atmosphere of stale familiarity'.

| 6/11 | Nature |
| 5/9 | Structure |

8 The pessimist still . . .
The reference to houses being cleared away in Weydon-Priors is the first real evidence of rural change occurring in the novel. It is a change which will also be reflected in the life of Henchard.

| 5/9 | Setting |
| 2/10 | Henchard |

9 A rather numerous . . .
The furmity woman makes four appearances in the novel, acting as a link between the changes that occur in Henchard's life. In her own ever-downward progress, she mirrors and forecasts the changing prospects in front of him. Here, in a reasonably respectable and prosperous tent, she presides over the momentous events which will set the story's action in motion. However, set as the tent is, in a village whose fortunes are on the decline, there is an ironic aspect to the freedom which Henchard will win from his wife.

| 8/10 | Setting |
| 7/17 | Structure |

10 The conversation took . . .
Henchard complains bitterly about marrying at an early age, being unable to find work and the thwarting of his ambitions. Notice how the auctioneer selling 'old horses' in the field outside acts as a lead-in to the auction of Susan. Another auction will feature as the background to an important moment later in the novel. Do you know what it is?

9/12	Setting
8/11	Henchard
0/11	Character

11 At the moment a . . .
The auction is interrupted when a swallow becomes trapped in the tent, distracting the assembled company. Would you agree that the bird's escape symbolizes Henchard's wish to be free of the responsibilities of his wife and child?

7/15	Nature
10/16	Character
10/12	Henchard

12 'Two guineas!' said . . .
In marked contrast to the normal pattern of an auction in the face of no bids over the initial five shillings, the auctioneer, instead of reducing the price proceeds to raise it. The auction with its emphasis on money and value reflects the changes which not only affect Henchard and Susan, but the great changes that are occurring in the relationship between rural and industrial life.

10/18	Setting
4/14	Susan
11/14	Henchard

13 All eyes were . . .
The sailor, arriving by chance at the crucial moment, enables the scene to be played out to its climax. He is a traveller, like so many of the characters—Lucetta, Farfrae, Elizabeth-Jane—whose travellings are a reflection of the turbulent movements and changes which are occurring in the society around them, and the great changes they will bring for Henchard.

| 1/18 | Fate |
| 0/34 | Newson |

14 The sailor looked . . .
Susan throws her wedding ring in the hay-trusser's face, symbolizing the end of their marriage. At this stage in the novel, you should be able to reach some tentative conclusions about the pressures which afflict Henchard and Susan, and their effects on them. Contrast the differences in the emotions they display.

12/16	Susan
12/16	Henchard

15 He rose and walked . . .
Notice how nature, in the twilight, the patient and loving horses, the setting of the sun, and the rosy cloud 'which seemed permanent, yet slowly changed' adds a feeling of intensity and almost inevitability to the dramatic nature of the recent happenings in the furmity woman's tent. There is a nice contrast here between the horses being auctioned with the later description of their lovingly caressing each other, and Henchard auctioning his wife and then falling into a drunken stupor.

11/48	Nature

16 'Mark me – I'll . . .'
Note the propriety way that Henchard refers to Elizabeth-Jane and his resolve that he won't go after Susan. There is a pervading sense of loneliness about Henchard which acts as a connecting thread throughout the narration of the story. You must consider to what extent this loneliness is brought about by his own foolhardiness, and the strange twists of chance and fate that beset him at every turn. In the morning he will have a different view of Susan's departure.

0/25	Loneliness
11/19	Character
14/20	Susan
14/17	Henchard

17 Perhaps from some little . . .
Notice how the last few lines of this chapter bring down a curtain, as it were, on the events that have just taken place. The furmity woman goes, to return some twenty years later to set in motion the next stage of the novel and mark the passage of yet more travellers.

9/21	Structure
16/19	Henchard

Chapter 2

18 Here the man . . .
As Henchard emerges from the tent he surveys a scene which is marked by remains of the ancient past: barrows and prehistoric forts. Of his own immediate past, his wife and daughter, the furmity woman, the sailor, the auctioneer and company, there is no sign. The future for Henchard is in his own hands – or maybe fate will take more of a hand than he expects!

13/26	Fate
12/23	Setting

19 'Did I tell . . .'
Henchard deeply regrets his actions of the previous night – or does he? There is an ambivalence, a contradictory aspect, in his wanting on the one hand to find his wife, and on the other worrying as to whether he mentioned his name to anybody. Do you agree? Is he more ashamed of his conduct, or of people knowing of his conduct? You need to consider his emotional state of mind as he searches for his wife and child. One part of him wants to find them but the other . . . ?

17/20	Henchard
16/20	Character

20 'Did I tell . . .'
Susan is described by Henchard as being free from levity of character –
always being very serious in her manner, of extreme simplicity of intellect
and meekness. To some extent these aspects of her character explain why
she believes there was some binding force in the sale of herself. However,
one shouldn't dismiss Susan's intellect too quickly. She does have the
presence of mind to keep her daughter's true parentage from Henchard in
the hope that she might gain some advantage for her daughter. Note also the
matter of the two anonymous notes that bring Elizabeth-Jane and Farfrae
together later in the novel. A great deal of deception occurs in the novel, and
for all sorts of reasons – be aware of it!

0/28	Deception
19/22	Character
16/25	Susan
19/21	Henchard

21 'Did I tell . . .'
Note how Henchard blames Susan for bringing him into disgrace at the end
of this paragraph. He is much concerned with the notion of his station in life
and his dignity. It is interesting to note that when he meets Susan again
some eighteen years later, he makes the same criticism of her!

17/42	Structure
20/22	Henchard

22 'I, Michael Henchard . . .'
Henchard takes an oath to avoid strong liquors; this is surely a clear
indication of the remorse he feels at his drunken action the previous day. For
this, he requires a 'fit place and imagery', revealing his superstitious nature.
However, this oath is no light promise to be broken at the least opportunity.
He means what he says. Elizabeth-Jane recognizes this trait in Henchard
when at the end of the novel, she fulfils the conditions that Henchard leaves
in his will.

20/23	Character
21/23	Henchard

23 When he had . . .
'The hay-trusser . . . seemed relieved at having made a start in a new
direction': notice how this feeling of a new direction is enhanced by Hardy's
use of natural setting. At every stage in the story the moods of the characters
and the dramatic events which affect them find a reflection in their natural
surroundings.

18/25	Setting
22/47	Character
22/24	Henchard

24 Weeks counted up . . .
Being 'shy' of revealing the true origins of his search for the sailor and
Susan, Henchard finds that it takes a great deal of time – perhaps it is a kind
of justification for the low-keyed nature of his search. How desperate do you
really feel he was to regain his wife and child?

23/31	Henchard

Chapter 3

25 The highroad into . . .
The arrival of Susan and Elizabeth-Jane at Weydon-Priors contrasts with
their arrival there, with Henchard, nineteen years earlier. They walk hand in
hand with a simple affection between them. The 'past-marked prospect'
(chapter 13) is a theme that haunts the pages of *The Mayor of Casterbridge*.
Everywhere we see the evidence of past civilizations and, for the characters,
reminders of both long-past and recent events. Henchard will pass this way
again at the end of the novel, but without a single member of his family to
comfort him in his loneliness and despair.

16/26	Loneliness
23/27	Setting
0/28	Elizabeth-Jane
20/26	Susan

26 The scene in . . .
Lonely figures on an open road is a symbol which recurs in the novel. What mood does this symbol evoke? Be aware of how frequently in the novel we meet the characters walking alone, to both chance and arranged meetings which will lead to momentous changes and occurrences in their lives.

18/50	Fate
25/72	Loneliness
25/28	Susan

27 Reaching the outskirts . . .
Hardy emphasizes the passing of time by noting the many social changes occurring in rural areas. Business at Weydon Fair had considerably dwindled, and there was evidence of the advance of civilization and the disturbance of the rural way of life. Some of the fair's roundabouts and other entertainments showed signs of mechanization.

25/36   Setting

28 'Why did we . . .'
Susan is trying to find Henchard now that the sailor Newson has been lost at sea. She has not told Elizabeth-Jane about her relationship to Henchard, thus ensuring that the various deceits, tragedies, and misunderstandings will follow from her desire to promote her daughter's well-being.

20/29   Deception
25/29   Elizabeth-Jane
26/29   Susan

29 The daughter looked . . .
As the fair has deteriorated so has the condition of the furmity woman. However, we see here the effect she has on Elizabeth-Jane who has a highly developed sense of what she considers to be respectable. Whilst no actual blood relation of Henchard, she does seem to mirror some of the ambitions to improve her lot which are such a driving force for Henchard. Equally, we see in her the results of Susan's dedicated desire to improve the lot of her daughter, even to the extent of misleading Henchard into accepting someone else's daughter as his own.

28/30   Deception
28/32   Elizabeth-Jane
28/33   Susan

30 'Ah, ma'am – well . . .'
The comment of the furmity woman that 'tis the sly and the underhand that get on in these times' is a curiously ironic though not strictly accurate comment on some of the deceits that occur during the unfolding of this story.

29/33   Deception

31 The hag reflected . . .
The old furmity seller has difficulty recalling the sale of a wife. Ironically, a few years later she demonstrates very clearly how well she remembers the events.

0/45   Irony
24/41   Henchard

32 Mrs Newson would . . .
Yet again Elizabeth-Jane returns to the theme of respectability, as she will do so on many other occasions.

29/35   Elizabeth-Jane

Chapter 4

33 But Susan Henchard's . . .
The author comments on the simplicity of Susan's belief that Newson had acquired a 'morally real and justifiable right to her'. It goes some way to explaining the reasons she went with him in the first place, and then stayed

30/37   Deception
29/34   Susan

with him. This simplicity does not stop her engaging in a long-term and ultimately disastrous deception of both Elizabeth-Jane and Henchard.

34 He then engaged . . .
Newson, already revealed as sympathetic and kindly, is further shown to be a man of great understanding of Susan's feelings. He recognizes her recent disillusionment at their relationship and immediately resolves to free her. Notice later in the book how he shows an understanding of the predicament that Henchard finds himself in when Newson suddenly arrives in search of Elizabeth-Jane.

33/35	Susan
13/63	Newson

35 The sight of . . .
Some of the agony through which Susan has gone is hinted at here. She has suffered personally, but what drives her on is a desire to assist 'the young mind of her companion [which] was struggling for enlargement'. At the same time we see how Elizabeth-Jane 'sought further into things than other girls in her position ever did'.

32/46	Elizabeth-Jane
34/36	Susan

36 At any rate . . .
In Susan's eyes there was no doubt as to the correctness of returning to Henchard, if he is still alive. Having no chance of advancement for her daughter in her present situation, her new-found awareness of the real bond between Newson and herself produced the circumstances which led to her taking the road again for Weydon-Priors.

27/38	Setting
35/37	Susan

37 At any rate . . .
Note the explanation given as to why she did not inform Elizabeth-Jane of the true nature of her origins.

33/66	Deception
36/39	Susan

38 'What an old-fashioned . . .'
Hardy gives a detailed description of Casterbridge, conveying the agricultural and pastoral character of the town and people.

36/40	Setting

39 'No, no, no!'
Susan's concern not to make too hasty an enquiry after Henchard, reinforces our awareness of her real reasons for travelling to find her husband – and it has nothing to do with love!

37/43	Susan

40 The agricultural and . . .
Note the detailed description of the trades carried on in Casterbridge, and how much the town depends on the countryside for its very existence.

38/42	Setting

41 'Oh, 'tis the . . .'
The two women heard Henchard's name mentioned. They now learn of the corn-factor who has sold the bakers grown wheat. Although the two are not yet linked, suspicion is created in our minds that there is a relationship. After a somewhat leisurely pace, the narrative begins to quicken.

31/43	Henchard

Chapter 5

42 The building before . . .
A common descriptive device used by Hardy is the framing of a scene by viewing it through a window or doorway. Look at other examples of this technique and the occasions on which it is used and see how it lends a unifying and linking aspect to events on either side of the 'framing'.

40/43	Setting
21/46	Structure

43 The interior . . .
How does this description of Henchard compare with that given in the first two chapters? Has Henchard changed in any particular way? Note how detailed description of clothing occurs throughout the novel. Clothing defines social position and here it contrasts the successful mayor with the skilled countryman of Susan's memories.

42/53	Setting
39/44	Susan
41/44	Henchard

44 'Yes, yes,' answered . . .
If Susan has searched for Henchard in order to secure a future for Elizabeth-Jane, why is she overwhelmed at finding him to be successful? Could it be she fears that his very success could put him beyond the half-laid plans she had in mind?

43/50	Susan
43/46	Henchard

45 A row of ancient . . .
The rustics add some humour to the narrative as well as being a vehicle for the description of Casterbridge society. They also serve, on occasion, to comment on the behaviour of their 'betters', and – as in the skimmington ride and the conflicting celebrations put on by Henchard and Farfrae later in the novel – help move the action of the narrative along. The use of dialect also helps to create the atmosphere of the rustic way of life, which is fast being subject to the changes being brought about by the upsurge of industrialization.

0/68	Rustics
31/62	Irony

46 'Another two year . . .'
We learn that nineteen years have passed since the sale of Henchard's wife. The oath has two years to run, yet in chapter 3 Hardy describes Elizabeth-Jane as a well-formed young woman of about eighteen. Does this apparent discrepancy have any significance with regard to the plot? There are a variety of clues as to the true identity of Elizabeth-Jane which the reader who gives close attention to the narrative may discover: the descriptions of her eyes at different parts of the novel and the author's references to 'her' rather than 'their' daughter when speaking of Susan and Henchard later in the novel.

42/50	Structure
35/50	Elizabeth-Jane
44/47	Henchard

47 This interruption about . . .
Look at how Henchard reacts to this public criticism. To what extent has he changed since we last met him? You should also look for evidence of those character traits which have remained unchanged.

46/48	Henchard
23/49	Character

48 'You must make . . .'
Dealing with the unpredictable effects of the weather and at times its seeming enmity is one of the great problems which besets the whole farming community, and particularly Henchard. However the chance criticism in a public place will set in motion events which rapidly bring together the main characters in the story.

15/61	Nature
47/49	Henchard

Chapter 6

	Characters and ideas previous/next comment

49 Now the group . . .
Yet again it is a stranger who moves into Henchard's life. Like the sailor Newson, he too is a traveller. Our first impression of Farfrae is of a young man of 'pleasant aspect'. In the pages and chapters to come you will need to consider the contrasts and similarities – if any – in their characters.

47/56   Character
48/50   Henchard
0/50   Farfrae

50 When he heard . . .
Note how the main characters are here drawn together: Elizabeth-Jane and Susan are drawn to the mayor because of their 'relationship', Farfrae is drawn to assist a man in trouble through no fault of his own. At the same time Farfrae brings himself to Elizabeth-Jane's notice, and by asking about a hotel ensures that they all end up at the same place.

26/54   Fate
46/51   Structure
46/52   Elizabeth-Jane
44/55   Susan
49/51   Farfrae
46/51   Henchard

51 'Give this to . . .'
Letters and notes occur throughout the novel giving shape and continuity to the plot. This note from Farfrae to Henchard results in Farfrae abandoning his voyage to America and staying on in Casterbridge as Henchard's manager. On what other occasions are letters or notes central to the action?

50/58   Structure
50/56   Farfrae
50/54   Henchard

52 As her mother . . .
Note again Elizabeth-Jane's concern with respectability. This time she judges Farfrae to be 'respectable' which leads her to suggest using the same inn at which to stay.

50/55   Elizabeth-Jane

53 Very few persons . . .
Notice the detailed description of the architecture of the Three Mariners. Hardy was a trained architect and such detail makes the urban setting more realistic.

43/64   Setting

54 Henchard stood without . . .
Note the irony of Henchard 'lowering the dignity of his presence' before entering the inn. It is this fateful meeting with Farfrae which will eventually lead to his downfall.

50/83   Fate
51/58   Henchard

Chapter 7

55 'I fear it is . . .'
Susan's far more practical approach to being respectable 'We must pay our way' is in contrast to her daughter's attitude.

52/56   Elizabeth-Jane
50/58   Susan

56 If there was . . .
Elizabeth-Jane is described as a person of natural kindness, willing to make self-sacrifices. You should look for evidence of this as the novel progresses. There is an ironic twist to her offer to help out at the inn. The respectability which she so desires is sacrificed to her willingness to help out in the inn so as to reduce their bill. This very act will later cause Henchard's wrath and drive him to doubt her 'respectability'.

49/65   Character
55/57   Elizabeth-Jane
51/57   Farfrae

57 'Tis the Scotch . . .'
Note this twist of fate which throws Elizabeth-Jane into Farfrae's company – even though he takes little notice of her.

56/59	Farfrae
56/69	Elizabeth-Jane

58 The meaning of . . .
The coincidence of the ladies being in the room next to Farfrae's, enables us to hear the conversation between the two men. Henchard has assumed that Farfrae was the man who had applied for the job as his manager. The chance arrival of Farfrae in Casterbridge at just this moment when Henchard was looking for a manager, and his obvious ability to fulfil the position, provides the impetus for the plot to develop.

51/60	Structure
55/66	Susan
54/59	Henchard

59 'I merely strolled . . .'
Note the conversation between the two men: the way in which Henchard tries to play down his interest in Farfrae's invention, and the openness and directness of approach adopted by Farfrae who could easily have charged a high premium for the information he gave to Henchard.

57/62	Farfrae
58/62	Henchard

60 'You're wrong!' said . . .
Who else in the novel stopped off in Casterbridge on their way to Bristol?

58/73	Structure

61 'Quite enough restored . . .'
The influence of natural events on the lives of man, especially in this rural community, is never far from our minds. There is no limit to the extent that nature may affect our lives, but our control over nature is severely limited.

48/118	Nature

62 'But hearken to me' . . .
Henchard offers Farfrae a job as manager of the corn branch. His plea to Farfrae to stay is ironic as the Scot is the one who will replace him as corn-factor and mayor. Later he will take Lucetta away from Henchard, and finally his daughter Elizabeth-Jane.

45/63	Irony
59/63	Henchard
59/64	Farfrae

63 Henchard paused. 'I . . .'
Note the irony here. Henchard previously gave all he had to a stranger in return for five guineas. In return for another 'bargain', he again puts all his worldly goods at the disposal of another stranger.

62/68	Irony
34/309	Newson
62/64	Henchard

64 Henchard again suspended . . .
Look at the assessment Henchard makes of the difference between his and Farfrae's attitudes to business. In what way would you say that Farfrae represented the new and Henchard the old way of life?

53/72	Setting
62/67	Farfrae
63/65	Henchard

65 'No, no; I . . .'
We discover that, although Henchard has been successful and has proved his strength by shouldering his responsibilities and keeping to his oath, he is still plagued by guilt.

56/66	Character
64/66	Henchard

Chapter 8

66 Thus they parted; . . .
Susan becomes more optimistic about a reunion with Henchard, when she overhears his avowal of shame for his past actions. To what extent are ambition – for herself or her daughter – and cunning, rather than love, her motives for seeking a reconciliation with Henchard?

37/79	Deception
65/70	Henchard
58/70	Susan
65/87	Character

67 There was a burst . . .
Farfrae performs with great effect, winning the hearts of the whole company of the Three Mariners. Why do you think Farfrae has such a strong effect on his audience?

64/69	Farfrae

68 'Danged if our . . .'
There is irony as well as humour in the remarks of Christopher Coney to Farfrae after he has sung one of his native songs. Note his and Buzzford's assessment of their town of Casterbridge.

45/119	Rustics
63/79	Irony

69 A general sense . . .
Elizabeth-Jane feels a sympathy for Farfrae. How do your own opinions of Farfrae's character compare with Elizabeth-Jane's first impressions?

57/71	Elizabeth-Jane
67/72	Farfrae

70 'We've made a . . .'
Note how well Susan seems to know her husband, accurately forecasting a future event.

66/76	Susan
66/72	Henchard

71 Elizabeth, who would . . .
Elizabeth-Jane returns to her theme of respectability.

69/75	Elizabeth-Jane

72 Meanwhile, the 'he' . . .
The 'framing' device which Hardy uses so often in the story this time seems to symbolize in the heartshaped holes in the window-shutters through which Henchard hears the Scot's song, not only the attraction which he feels towards Farfrae, but also the loneliness of Henchard. There is a stark contrast here between the lonely Henchard on one side of the shutter and Farfrae on the other side, the stranger in Casterbridge who has won the hearts of his companions in the Three Mariners.

26/96	Loneliness
64/74	Setting
69/75	Farfrae
70/82	Henchard

Chapter 9

73 When Elizabeth-Jane . . .
The scene is now set for the various developments that will take place in the plot. September in Weydon-Priors, where Henchard held centre-stage for a short while and destroyed his family, has given way to September in Casterbridge where again he holds centre-stage, as Mayor. Here, however, the events will be of much greater moment, though closely linked with those occurring at Weydon-Priors so many years ago.

60/81	Structure

74 When Elizabeth-Jane . . .
Note how the town of Casterbridge and the surrounding rural life

72/78	Setting

complement each other, and how Hardy conveys this in the novel by contrasting natural and urban settings.

75 'He was a good . . .'
Farfrae leaves the Three Mariners and although he glances at Elizabeth-Jane he looks away without nodding, smiling or saying a word. What is her reaction to this slight?

71/81 Elizabeth-Jane
72/81 Farfrae

76 While they debated . . .
Is the thoughtful reader being given a clue here by Susan referring to 'her' daughter and not 'their' daughter?

70/77 Susan

77 'In that case' . . .
The afterthought '–or *me*.' suggests that Susan suddenly realizes Henchard may wish to discover more of their lives without the presence of Elizabeth-Jane. What could be in her mind do you think?

76/95 Susan

78 It was about . . .
A writer may clarify a character or situation by referring to a similar character or incident known to the reader. Hardy refers to the Greek muse of song and dance, Terpsichore, to give colour to his description of the streets of Casterbridge on a market day.

74/80 Setting

79 The yeomen, farmers, . . .
There is an irony in the statement 'Chicanery, subterfuge, had hardly a place in the streets of this honest borough'. Certainly this description does not apply very accurately to the lives of some of the characters in this novel. Can you list any such incidents which contradict this statement?

68/82 Irony
66/98 Deception

80 Thus Casterbridge was . . .
Why do you think that all townsfolk are affected by changes in the fortunes of the farming community?

78/93 Setting

81 Elizabeth turned the . . .
Notice how this chapter is structured. We left the two men at the beginning of the chapter, with Farfrae apparently departing for America. Then to Elizabeth-Jane's and our surprise, we find him working at Henchard's 'like a man who permanently ruled there'. It is not until the end of the chapter that we discover the conversation that occurred between the two men on the road out of town.

73/89 Structure
75/90 Elizabeth-Jane
75/83 Farfrae

82 'Well, here's success . . .'
Notice the irony of Henchard wishing Farfrae well, and how he 'shall often think' of the help he received from Farfrae.

79/91 Irony
72/84 Henchard

83 'I never expected . . .'
Farfrae declares that Henchard's offer is the work of providence. Can you find another occasion when Farfrae's actions are determined by what he calls providence?

54/106 Fate
81/84 Farfrae

84 The face of Mr Henchard . . .
Notice the impulsive nature of Mr Henchard – 'Now you are my friend!'.
After such a short acquaintance he has given him a major responsibility for
his corn business, taken him into his own home, and elevated him virtually
to the position that a life-long friend and confidant would occupy. However,
is the trust he puts in Farfrae ever abused or taken advantage of?

Chapter 10

85 While she still . . .
Note the biblical allusion to the 'quicker cripple at Bethesda' which Hardy
uses to illustrate and comment on Joshua Jopp's entrance to the corn-factor's
office. In the Bible, the first cripple into the pool at Bethesda after it had been
disturbed by an angel, was cured. Jopp was obviously anxious to lay claim to
'his' job when he stepped past Elizabeth-Jane into Henchard's offce. Why
do you think such biblical allusions may be more difficult to understand now
than when the novel was written?

86 'Well, you are . . .'
Do you think that Henchard's treatment of Joshua Jopp was justified? It
throws some light on his attitude to running a business, as well as giving an
insight into the nature of the man. Be aware of how this incident influences
Jopp's actions in the future.

87 This at once . . .
Note how the first thought of Henchard on hearing the news of Susan's
appearance with a daughter was relief and thankfulness that Susan had not
broadcast his actions to the world at large and more particularly to Elizabeth-
Jane. It gives an indication of an ever-present guilt which he obviously still
felt many years after the event.

88 It was with . . .
Elizabeth-Jane is surprised at the 'gentle delicacy' of Henchard's manner; it
contrasted strongly with his abrupt and unmannerly treatment of Jopp. The
dining-room into which he takes her reflects much of the physical character
of the man, with its heavy mahogany furniture the legs of which are 'shaped
like those of an elephant', and the huge volumes of religious works.

89 He sat down . . .
Would you agree that Henchard demonstrates his concern for the well-being
of his wife and daughter by enclosing five pounds with the note to Susan?
What is the significance of the five shillings which he adds as an
afterthought? Hardy makes a comment on this himself later in the chapter.

90 He took her hand . . .
Note the reference to her 'aerial-grey eyes'. How were they described earlier
in the story, near the middle of chapter 1, when she was a baby?

Characters and ideas	
previous/next comment	
83/103	Farfrae
82/86	Henchard
0/86	Joshua Jopp
85/223	Joshua Jopp
84/87	Henchard
86/88	Henchard
66/108	Character
87/89	Henchard
81/92	Structure
88/90	Henchard
81/121	Elizabeth-Jane
89/91	Henchard

91 'Begad!' he suddenly . . .

This is a strange reaction, to suddenly worry whether the two women were imposters, especially after his obvious acceptance of the new arrivals into his life. It is a little like his unquestioning acceptance of Farfrae. What is so ironic though, is that one is an imposter, though not knowingly so, as is discovered later. The irony is increased when he found 'a something in Elizabeth [which] soon assured him' that she was his daughter and only her mother's identity now needed settling!

90/92	Henchard
82/92	Irony

92 'It never rains . . .'

Henchard's interest in Farfrae is overshadowed by the arrival of Susan and Elizabeth-Jane. He now has within the space of a day, a new manager, his wife returned, and a grown daughter. It is small wonder that he remarks 'It never rains but it pours!', though is this an appropriate saying to encompass such overwhelming joys as appear to be descending upon Henchard, or is it more like prophetic irony? It is certainly the end of the relatively simple life for the Mayor of Casterbridge where virtually his only concern was the running of his business, and where his vow not to drink liquor kept him clear of possible problems. However, even there the temptation will return – the term of his vow is shortly to expire. From what you know of Henchard's character so far, do you think he is going to find it easy to control the course of his life in the future?

91/110	Irony
89/96	Structure
91/93	Henchard

93 'Meet me at . . .'

A 'past-marked prospect', the Ring on the Budmouth Road will form the background for Henchard's meeting with Susan. Why do you think he makes this arrangement rather than inviting her to his house?

80/94	Setting
92/95	Henchard

Chapter 11

94 The Ring at Casterbridge . . .

The novel is placed in historical perspective by reference to Roman remains. Note the gloomy yet strangely relevant detail that speaks of skeletons being dug up in and around Casterbridge. The skeleton from Henchard's past is about to confront him and his actions.

93/95	Setting

95 The Amphitheatre was . . .

Note the 'Melancholy, impressive, lonely', nature of the spot; how intrigues were arranged there, meetings after 'divisions and feuds'. It is surely a comment on this meeting between Susan and Henchard and the quality of their relationship that one kind of appointment seldom had a place there – 'that of happy lovers'.

94/96	Setting
77/98	Susan
92/97	Henchard

96 Some boys had . . .

The Ring at Casterbridge is used later in the novel for another meeting – between whom and in what circumstances? Do you think it makes a sympathetic or a constrasting background for these meetings?

72/105	Loneliness
95/99	Setting
92/106	Structure

97 Henchard had chosen . . .
There is a comment later in the novel to the effect that if Henchard's actions in the past had not been kept such a close secret and known about much sooner, his fellow businessmen and the townsfolk would likely have looked upon the adventure as the excesses of youth and largely dismissed it from consideration. However, his secrecy on the matter, which started in chapter 2, when he was so concerned as to whether he had disclosed his name, now catches up with him. 'As Mayor of the town, with a reputation to keep up', his deception along with those of other characters is a major factor in the events which lead to his downfall.

95/98   Henchard

98 Just before eight . . .
The lack of necessity for speech, Henchard supporting Susan in his arms, his first words mentioning his abstinence from drink, her bowed head in unspoken acknowledgement and acceptance of his admission and repentance, all speak of reconciliation, understanding and love. However, Hardy's description of the Ring as no place where happy lovers meet, but as a place of intrigue, is soon to see fulfilment. Both Susan and Henchard agree to deceive Elizabeth-Jane about her parenthood, but Susan's is a double deceit which involves her in lying to Henchard. Whatever the underlying reasons for deceit, it is hardly a good basis on which to build the future.

79/100   Deception
95/99   Susan
97/100   Henchard

99 'O Michael! because . . .'
Susan believed that although she was not legally married to Newson, there was something solemn and binding in the bargain. The fact that Newson had paid for her in good faith was enough to make her believe that she owed him faithfulness. Remember how near the end of chapter 2 Henchard criticized Susan–'didn't she know better than bring me into this disgrace!'? Has he really altered in his attitude to her since then, given his comment 'But–to lead me into this!'?

96/103   Setting
98/100   Susan

100 'Well–we must . . .'
Neither Henchard nor Susan wish Elizabeth-Jane to know the truth about the past. Why is this? Are their reasons for deceiving her the same?

98/109   Deception
99/101   Susan
98/102   Henchard

101 'I am quite . . .'
Note how Susan confirms the driving force behind her return to Henchard: the welfare of Elizabeth-Jane. Would she really be content 'for herself' to leave immediately and never bother him again? What does this say about her as a person?

100/102   Susan

102 'Right,' said Henchard . . .
Has Susan forgiven her husband? Certainly, her response leaves the matter in some doubt, as indeed there would seem to be some doubt that Henchard really loves Susan in the truest sense of the word. Their parting exchange seems to bear out Hardy's statement that only rarely do lovers meet at the Ring.

101/114   Susan
100/103   Henchard

Chapter 12

103 He stood behind . . .
Farfrae shows great skill at sorting out the corn-factor's paperwork. Henchard is 'mentally and physically unfit' for such work. Note the tremendous contrast in their attitudes to the business. Henchard is very much the traditional, rustic businessman working by rule of thumb and instinct. Farfrae is more the product and representative of a new way of life and business.

104 Donald had wished . . .
Farfrae shows a good deal of sensitivity in speedily recognizing the strengths and weaknesses in Henchard's character.

105 'It is odd,' . . .
Henchard again returns to the fact of his loneliness, mentioned most recently at the end of chapter 8. Success in business and his position of Mayor of Casterbridge does nothing to alleviate that loneliness, indeed, perhaps it is part of its cause. He feels the need to confide his problems in Farfrae – barely the day after he had met him. Consider the great emotional turmoil that Henchard has gone through in the last day or so, and how he is reacting to it. What do we learn about Henchard's character from this act of confidence in Farfrae?

106 'That's what I've . . .'
Suddenly, we learn something new about Henchard's life, and how 'by doing right with Susan I wrong another innocent woman'. At the moment of what should have been supreme happiness a cloud appears on the horizon.

107 'Ah, no, I never . . .'
Contrast this interesting disclosure of Farfrae's view of life with that which Henchard has just mentioned.

108 'They are! For . . .'
Henchard shows his willingness to accept responsibility for his past in wishing to make amends to both Susan and Lucetta. Note how even more closely he draws Farfrae into his personal affairs by asking him to write the letter to the 'young lady' in Jersey.

109 'I think I'd run . . .'
Farfrae's advice to tell the truth is rejected by Henchard, and his act of rejection forewarns us of his future behaviour. Instead of taking Elizabeth-Jane into their confidences, Henchard and Susan will play out this elaborate charade of meeting and courting 'to keep our child's respect', the very thing that Henchard will lose. Note how we have already seen the great store that Elizabeth-Jane puts in people's respect and being respectable.

110 When he had gone . . .
Henchard's musings as he returns from posting his letter are shortly to receive their answer. Note the irony here: he disposed of Susan for five guineas, but she returned. He now hopes to dispose of the other woman in his life, with a payment.

Characters and ideas previous/next comment		
99/112	Setting	
84/104	Farfrae	
102/104	Henchard	
103/105	Henchard	
103/107	Farfrae	
96/146	Loneliness	
104/106	Henchard	
83/112	Fate	
96/110	Structure	
105/107	Henchard	
104/109	Farfrae	
106/108	Henchard	
107/113	Henchard	
87/113	Character	
100/114	Deception	
107/127	Farfrae	
92/115	Irony	
106/111	Structure	

111 'Can it be . . .'
Notice how we are kept in suspense at the close of the chapter. Will the letter of explanation and the money signify the end of the matter?

110/124	Structure

Chapter 13

112 The cottage which . . .
The mood of the chapter is set by a description of the autumnal evening sun and of the historical remains that surround the cottage Henchard has hired for Susan. 'The usual touch of melancholy that a past-marked prospect lends' is perhaps an appropriate image to accompany the cottage which Henchard hires for his wife, bearing in mind events to come. Can you find other instances where a mood is set by a description of the sun?

103/113	Setting

113 As soon as . . .
The superficial conversations he has with Susan in order not to seem too familiar in front of Elizabeth-Jane amuse Henchard. We are reminded of his laugh which was 'not encouraging to strangers' (see chapter 5); certainly Susan does not find it amusing. Note also the description of his actions as the 'course of strict mechanical rightness . . . at any expense to the later one [the woman from Jersey] and to his own sentiments'. How much does this say about his attitudes towards these two women, his daughter and his view of his social and moral responsibilities to them all?

112/126	Setting
108/115	Henchard
108/117	Character

114 The poor woman . . .
Susan is concerned about the deception of Elizabeth-Jane. What do you think Susan fears most about revealing the past to her daughter? Note also the references to 'her' girl's reputation; Henchard has no part in Elizabeth-Jane.

109/132	Deception
102/116	Susan

115 'Not at all,' . . .
Note the prophetic irony of Henchard's remark that he will soon be able to leave everything to Farfrae and that he will have more time to call his own.

110/148	Irony
113/117	Henchard

116 Henchard's visits here . . .
What is ironic, and apt in the town boys referring to Susan as 'The Ghost'?

114/125	Susan

117 He pressed on . . .
Although Henchard wants to make amends to Susan and provide a home for Elizabeth-Jane, his third resolve is to punish himself. How will he do this, and what does the punishment involved suggest about his character?

115/120	Henchard
113/120	Character

118 Susan Henchard entered . . .
The marriage of Henchard and Susan is not a very exciting event and the mood is conveyed by the description of the weather.

61/139	Nature

119 'Tis five-and-forty . . .'
The discussions of the townsfolk present at the wedding provide humour, but also suggest future difficulties in the relationship of Henchard and Susan.

68/160   Rustics

Chapter 14

120 A Martinmas summer . . .
Henchard showed great kindness to Susan 'as a man, mayor and churchwarden could' – but did he as a husband and lover? Why do you think he found it impossible to love her? Does he even now blame her for going off with Newson and his ensuing, albeit self-inflicted, loss of dignity?

117/124   Henchard
117/133   Character

121 To Elizabeth-Jane . . .
Yet again a reference to Elizabeth-Jane's 'grey' eyes. As yet neither the reader nor Henchard are aware of her true parentage, but the author has been hinting that there is yet another mystery to be unfolded.

90/122   Elizabeth-Jane

122 It might have been . . .
The affluent life which Elizabeth-Jane was now able to live made it possible for her to develop. How does her concern with clothes reveal certain aspects of her character and attitude to life?

106/123   Fate
121/123   Elizabeth-Jane

123 'I won't be too . . .'
Farfrae, too, referred to 'providence' when accepting the job as manager from Henchard. Are either of these gifts from Providence as free as they seem or do they include a debt which has yet to be paid?

122/139   Fate
122/128   Elizabeth-Jane

124 The three members . . .
What implications do Henchard's observation of the changed colour of Elizabeth-Jane's hair have for the development of the plot? There have been other references hinting at a mystery here. Note how a few paragraphs on there is a mention of Susan's unease about the question 'to which the future held the key'.

111/148   Structure
120/127   Henchard

125 Then Mrs Henchard . . .
The mystery surrounding Elizabeth-Jane is compounded by Susan's reaction to Henchard's suggestion that Elizabeth-Jane's surname should be changed to Henchard. Why should she object to such a change? Note also the clever way she prevails upon her daughter to reject the suggestion. Susan is certainly not just a simple, meek nonentity.

116/148   Susan

126 Meanwhile the great . . .
Farfrae's new ideas in managing the corn trade enable it to thrive, but 'the rugged picturesqueness of the old method disappeared with its inconveniences'.

113/129   Setting

127 The position of . . .
Although Henchard has little respect for Farfrae's physical strength he admires the man's intellectual abilities. What other contrasts between their characters can you make? Note the prophetic image of Henchard almost supported by Farfrae's slight figure. We will see later in the novel for just what exactly Henchard will have to thank, and curse, Farfrae.

128 Her quiet eye . . .
It is through the discerning eye of Elizabeth-Jane that we begin to see much of the action. Hardy identifies her with the view of the narrator. It is through Elizabeth-Jane's natural insight that we see Henchard's affection for Farfrae, his tendency to domineer and the suggestion of a possible rift between the two men in the future.

129 Casterbridge, as has been . . .
The importance of the corn trade to the town of Casterbridge is suggested by a description of the integration of urban and rural settings.

130 Henchard, as was . . .
Elizabeth-Jane and Farfrae are brought together at the Durnover Hill granary having both received similar notes. Given the obvious affection in which Henchard holds both of them, it would seem not unreasonable that he should try to bring them together – or is it someone else's doing?

131 Acting on this . . .
Examine the reactions of these two people to their meeting. Were they really as calm as some of their conversation suggests? What would have been the effect on the two of them of Farfrae delicately blowing dust and husks off 'her back hair, and her side hair, and her neck, and the crown of her bonnet, and the fur of her victorine', and Elizabeth-Jane saying 'O, thank you,' at every puff? Note Farfrae's reaction as Elizabeth-Jane leaves.

Chapter 15

132 But Donald Farfrae . . .
Elizabeth-Jane discovers she is attractive to others. Her new clothes bring her the admiration of the townsfolk, but ironically she is afraid of posing as someone she is not.

133 The unhappy Whittle . . .
How does the argument over Henchard's treatment of Abel Whittle reveal a sharp contrast between the characters of Henchard and Farfrae? Can you see some humour in the situation? Was Farfrae being perhaps too sensitive?

134 ''Tis not tyrannical!' . . .
Do you consider that Henchard's treatment of Abel Whittle shows him to be unfair? If so, what is the explanation for the fact that he kept Abel's mother in coals and snuff all the previous winter?

Characters and ideas		
previous/next comment		
109/130	Farfrae	
124/133	Henchard	
123/130	Elizabeth-Jane	
126/153	Setting	
128/131	Elizabeth-Jane	
127/131	Farfrae	
130/132	Elizabeth-Jane	
130/133	Farfrae	
114/154	Deception	
131/140	Elizabeth-Jane	
131/136	Farfrae	
127/134	Henchard	
120/137	Character	
0/134	Abel Whittle	
133/135	Henchard	
133/260	Abel Whittle	

135 Morally he was . . .
Consider this conversation with the child. Are the opinions of the townspeople fair? Note how Henchard reacts to their criticisms.

134/136   Henchard

136 They parted thus . . .
Why do you think Henchard regrets having revealed the secrets of his life to Farfrae? Why does he think of Farfrae with 'dim dread'? Is he justified in his fears?

135/137   Henchard
133/137   Farfrae

Chapter 16

137 On this account . . .
Henchard's attitude to Farfrae becomes more reserved and he is too courteous. However, do you think the description of Henchard's friendship for Farfrae as being 'mechanized' was a fair one?

133/140   Character
136/138   Henchard
136/142   Farfrae

138 He had grown . . .
Henchard worries that he 'would sink to the position of second fiddle'. Is there to some extent almost a wish for self-destruction in Henchard's character? Note how he always seems to make the wrong decision or to make the right decision too late.

137/139   Henchard

139 Everybody applauded . . .
Although the rift between Henchard and Farfrae is largely a result of Henchard's actions, fate intervenes in the form of bad weather, making a complete failure of his entertainments. Was it only the bad weather that prevented the townspeople from coming, or was it that they were beginning to feel some sort of loyalty to Farfrae? Certainly, in the rival entertainments we see a foreshadowing of the different paths they will take and the degrees of success they will achieve.

123/149   Fate
118/217   Nature
138/141   Henchard

140 All the town . . .
Hardy refers to the Italian painter Correggio in order to describe the light in Elizabeth-Jane's eyes as she watches Farfrae dancing. What does the allusion help to say about her?

137/141   Character
132/144   Elizabeth-Jane

141 All the town . . .
Perhaps appropriately, Henchard walks in the shadows of Farfrae's celebrations. How do the remarks of the townsfolk affect Henchard's reaction to Farfrae's festivities and what does this tell us about his character?

140/142   Character
139/142   Henchard

142 The young man . . .
The rift between Henchard and Farfrae is complete when Farfrae is dismissed as manager. Is Farfrae's reaction to the dismissal consistent with what we know of his character?

141/144   Character
141/143   Henchard
137/144   Farfrae

143 Henchard went home . . .
At the beginning of the story, Henchard, drunk and sorry for himself 'dismissed' his wife and child from his life. They have returned and set in

142/146   Henchard

train events that will prove catastrophic for Henchard. Now, drunk again with jealousy and self-pity he dismisses Farfrae from his employ, but it is an action he will live to regret. Note how here, as before, he regrets the actions of the previous night.

Chapter 17

144 'I wish I was . . .'
Elizabeth-Jane realizes that she is in love with Farfrae, but, although he comes close to proposing to her he decides that the time is not suitable. How do Farfrae's actions suggest he is of a calculating nature? His judgment of what is right in relation to his dealings with other people need to be looked at carefully, especially where his personal feelings are involved.

142/145	Character
142/150	Farfrae
140/145	Elizabeth-Jane

145 The next day . . .
Note the effect that Farfrae is having on Elizabeth-Jane. Is he encouraging her in any way, or are her feelings merely those of an immature and inexperienced girl?

144/146	Character
144/147	Elizabeth-Jane

146 His friends of the . . .
Henchard's jealousy, impulsiveness and temper which have caused the rift with his friend and manager, now isolate him from the community which does not share his feelings of enmity towards Farfrae.

105/151	Loneliness
145/157	Character
143/149	Henchard

147 She hesitated for . . .
Once before Elizabeth-Jane agreed to a course of action, then under pressure from Susan – can you remember what it was? Now she is pressured by Henchard to reject Farfrae. Is she a very weak character, or a victim of circumstances?

145/166	Elizabeth-Jane

148 Sir, – I make . . .
Henchard sends a note to Farfrae requesting that he does not see Elizabeth-Jane. Ironically, as Hardy points out, if Henchard were to encourage him to be his son-in-law it could possibly heal the rift between them. Note how Susan, despite her feelings on the matter, has no part to play in this affair.

115/150	Irony
124/152	Structure
125/152	Susan

149 But most probably . . .
'Character is Fate' Hardy noted in his diary 'It is not improbabilities of incident but improbabilities of character that matter'. To what extent do you think aspects of Henchard's character caused the split with Farfrae? Did events beyond his control have any influence? Is Henchard without a 'light' to guide him to a better way? Consider how he has managed over the many years since selling his wife to climb the ladder of success, and the possibility that now his wife and daughter have returned and he is repaying them for his actions in the past, he no longer has the spur of guilt to drive him on.

146/150	Henchard
139/168	Fate

150 A time came . . .
Note the physical imagery involved in describing the conflict between Henchard and Farfrae. It is a commercial conflict which Farfrae will surely win. The irony lies in the physical nature of the imagery which 'speaks' of

148/151	Irony
144/177	Farfrae
149/155	Henchard

the actual bodily conflict that will involve the two men at a later date, when Henchard will win – in the physical sense – but Farfrae will win morally.

151 Almost every Saturday . . .
In order to emphasize Henchard's isolation and loneliness, Hardy refers to the mythical hero Bellerophon, who, deserted by the gods, wandered alone facing many hazardous tasks.

150/162	Irony
146/165	Loneliness

Chapter 18

152 Her mother was . . .
Note how conveniently Susan is about to die, as Lucetta is brought to the fore. With this sequence of events, an enormous number of other conflicts are made possible in the relationships between the characters Elizabeth-Jane, Lucetta, Farfrae and Henchard.

148/154	Structure
0/155	Lucetta
148/158	Susan

153 Elizabeth, who had . . .
Note how the description of Henchard looking at the letter from Lucetta – 'a vista of past enactments' – conjures up the phrase 'past-marked prospects'. Here we have the integration of past history with present events, the ever-present embodiments of the past in ancient barrows and other remains, the ever-present reminder of Henchard's past in Susan and Elizabeth-Jane, and now another figure from what he thought was his past comes back to haunt him – Lucetta.

129/161	Setting

154 The writer said . . .
A note arrives from Lucetta forgiving Henchard for the dilemma he has placed her in and requesting the return of certain letters. Note how she recognizes that there was no deceit on his part about Susan's return and that the only course open to him was to remarry Susan. Is the only time of importance that Henchard had been totally without deceit when he took Farfrae's advice about what to say in his letter to Lucetta?

132/155	Deception
152/156	Structure

155 'Now you will . . .'
Henchard is about to agree to yet another secret about the past, this time with Lucetta. A web of intrigue and deception is being woven.

154/164	Deception
152/156	Lucetta
150/156	Henchard

156 'I am now on . . .'
Lucetta fails to keep the appointment she made, much to Henchard's relief. Who else was on their way to Bristol but eventually settled in Casterbridge?

154/158	Structure
155/179	Lucetta
155/157	Henchard

157 Henchard breathed heavily.
Henchard considers how he 'ought' to marry Lucetta if the chance occurs. Is there any element of desire, passion, or love, in the conclusion he has just drawn?

156/163	Henchard
146/165	Character

Characters and ideas
previous/next comment

158 *'Mr Michael Henchard.'*
Susan's letter will be opened at the wrong time by Henchard. Lucetta's letters will also be opened at the wrong time and by the wrong man later in the novel – both events leading to tragic consequences.

156/159   Structure
152/161   Susan

159 A word from . . .
The mystery of the notes which were sent to Elizabeth-Jane and Farfrae is solved when Susan reveals that she sent them in order to bring her daughter and Farfrae together.

158/168   Structure

160 At the town-pump . . .
The gossip of the rustics round the town pump add humour and pathos to the sombre occasion of Susan's death.

119/297   Rustics

161 'And she was as white . . .'
Susan, like Henchard, is a superstitious person. The four one-pennies were to be used as weights to close her eyes after she had died. The superstitious belief was that if a person's eyes remained open they became a ghost.

153/170   Setting
158/162   Susan

162 'Well, poor soul . . .'
Note the irony of 'her wishes and ways will all be as nothing!' Perhaps the least forceful of the main characters, two of her main desires are fulfilled: she brings her daughter into the safekeeping of Henchard's house, and whilst she is not to see it, Elizabeth-Jane does indeed marry Farfrae.

151/181   Irony
161/192   Susan

Chapter 19

163 Henchard's wife was . . .
Is this assessment by Henchard sufficiently full? Is he a man able to look at himself and his actions with any degree of reasonable self-analysis? He wonders whether he ought to tell Elizabeth-Jane of her true father or leave 'well alone'. Has he ever been able to do this?

157/164   Henchard

164 'She should have . . .'
How well could Henchard's criticism of Susan have been equally applied to his own situation?

163/165   Henchard
155/171   Deception

165 'She should have . . .'
Henchard, driven by loneliness and his need to express love, reveals that he and not Newson is Elizabeth-Jane's father.

151/170   Loneliness
164/166   Henchard
157/171   Character

166 She tried to . . .
Note how despite her effort to 'confront him trustfully', Elizabeth-Jane was still 'troubled at his presence'. Something worries her – can you think what it might be? It lies in the conflict in her mind over the respective claims of the man she knew as her father, Newson, and this man who claims to be her father.

147/172   Elizabeth-Jane
165/167   Henchard

167 'I don't want . . .'
Note the image of the 'great tree in a wind'. Henchard, buffeted by the cruel chances of fate and the results of his own actions, is desperate to strengthen his hold on Elizabeth-Jane.

166/168   Henchard

168 My Dear Michael . . .
Ironically, Henchard's search for proof of Elizabeth-Jane's parentage leads him to the badly sealed letter from Susan, in which he discovers that his own child died and that Elizabeth-Jane is Newson's daughter. Note Henchard's reactions to this discovery of the letter's contents – as though the letter were a 'window-pane through which he saw for miles'. Suddenly, but too late, past actions of Susan become clear to him.

159/182   Structure
167/169   Henchard

169 Misery taught him . . .
Henchard's superstitious nature makes him believe that there is a 'sinister intelligence' punishing him for his past actions. How does Henchard react to the misery of these events?

168/218   Fate
168/171   Henchard

170 This ironical sequence . . .
How is Henchard's loneliness and suffering reflected by the mood of his walk along the river bank? Look at the words and images used: 'mournful phases', 'torturing cramps', 'pined', 'slow, noiseless, and dark', 'voice of desolation', 'the corpse of a man'.

165/177   Loneliness
161/178   Setting

171 'I have thought . . .'
Elizabeth-Jane accepts Henchard as her father and he decides that it is necessary to carry on the deception. Note, though, his realization of the ruin of all his plans and expectations. What is now left to him to make his life worth living?

164/193   Deception
169/172   Henchard
165/172   Character

Chapter 20

172 Of all the enigmas . . .
Henchard is cold in his manner towards Elizabeth-Jane, picking fault in her use of dialect words and lack of learning. What light does this shed on his character? Would you say that he is a changed man as a result of all his disappointments, or does his character not change at all? Can any blame be apportioned to Elizabeth-Jane for the situation in which she finds herself?

166/173   Elizabeth-Jane
171/174   Character
171/174   Henchard

173 She started the pen . . .
Hardy alludes to the Roman goddess Minerva who was considered to be a very masculine woman, to describe Elizabeth-Jane's mistake in learning bold hand instead of 'ladies'-hand'.

172/176   Elizabeth-Jane

174 Henchard glanced at . . .
Susan's fears that the mayor's pride would be damaged (see chapter 8), if he discovered that Elizabeth-Jane had worked at the Three Mariners, are confirmed when Nance Mockridge reveals the incident to Henchard.

172/188   Character
172/175   Henchard

175 Nance glanced triumphantly . . .
Despite the insolence of Nance Mockridge, Henchard says nothing about discharging her. What makes him so sensitive about such issues?

174/180   Henchard

176 Convinced of the . . .
Elizabeth-Jane fails to understand the reasons for Henchard's hostility towards her. She is ashamed of her lack of learning and strives hard to remedy this.

173/177   Elizabeth-Jane

177 Thus she lived on . . .
Elizabeth-Jane lives a lonely life, repressing her interest in Farfrae who never seems to notice her. Consider the life she now leads. Do you consider it strange that Farfrae should make no attempt to see her?

170/201   Loneliness
176/179   Elizabeth-Jane
150/182   Farfrae

178 Winter had almost . . .
It is perhaps ironic that Susan's grave is now part of the 'past-marked prospect'.

170/179   Setting

179 There, approaching her . . .
What can we say about the characters of Lucetta and Elizabeth-Jane from the contrast in the way they dress?

178/184   Setting
156/188   Lucetta
177/186   Elizabeth-Jane

180 Interesting as things . . .
Henchard's fortunes continue to decline. His period as Mayor of Caster-bridge is about to end, and he discovers he will not be invited to become an alderman. The annoyance that Farfrae will be so invited is further heightened by the knowledge, recently obtained, that it was Farfrae whom Elizabeth-Jane had served at the Three Mariners.

175/181   Henchard

181 Ever since the . . .
The arrival of Susan and Elizabeth-Jane in Casterbridge promised to be a happy reunion, but ironically their appearance contained the seeds of Henchard's downfall. The dinner at the King's Head was his 'Austerlitz'. It was at Austerlitz that Napoleon defeated the armies of Austria and Russia, but it also marked the beginning of his fall from power.

162/218   Irony
180/182   Henchard

182 Sir, – On consideration . . .
Henchard writes to Farfrae to tell him that he no longer wishes to interfere with his courtship of Elizabeth-Jane. What is the reason given here for him changing his mind? Can you explain the reference to Farfrae's sudden appearance at the churchyard gate? Is it mere coincidence?

168/183   Structure
177/195   Farfrae
181/186   Henchard

183 'What is your history?'
Note the strong parallels here with earlier incidents. Henchard confided his story to a complete stranger, but unwittingly left out key elements of the story. Elizabeth-Jane does the same. Both the people confided in turn out to be eventual rivals; Farfrae for Henchard's business, Lucetta for Farfrae's hand. Farfrae immediately moves into Henchard's house, Elizabeth-Jane moves in with Lucetta.

182/185   Structure

Chapter 21

184 The position of . . .
Note how aspects of Lucetta's past are suggested by the architectural description and historical setting of High-Place Hall.

185 Had she watched . . .
A link between Henchard and Lucetta is suggested by the mayor's mysterious visit to High-Place Hall creating suspense which is resolved at the end of the chapter.

186 'Father, have you any . . .'
Note the absolute indifference of Henchard's response. If he is really so indifferent to her going, why doesn't he complete the break between them by telling her about Newson?

187 'It had better be . . .'
Does Henchard really think that by giving Elizabeth-Jane money he will resolve his moral obligations to her? Note how he also tried the same approach with both Susan and Lucetta.

188 The lady seemed . . .
Why do you suppose that Lucetta shows concern when Elizabeth-Jane says that she has not told her father to where she is moving.

189 But the proposal . . .
Henchard's impulsiveness again gets him into trouble. When he sees the efforts Elizabeth-Jane has made to improve herself, he regrets having spoken roughly to her and asks her to stay, but once again he shows his love too late. Whilst we have not been told in so many words, it is obvious from Henchard's reaction to the knowledge of where Elizabeth-Jane is going to stay that he knew who else was at High-Place Hall.

Chapter 22

190 My dear Mr Henchard, . . .
By means of yet another letter we are acquainted with Lucetta's plan to marry Henchard.

191 He was in . . .
Henchard needs to fill the place in his emotions left empty by the loss of Elizabeth-Jane, but what is his main reason for wanting to marry Lucetta? What are Lucetta's reasons for wanting to marry Henchard?

192 'I am in residence' . . .
It is interesting to note that, just like Susan, Lucetta had acquired a new surname. Are there other parallels in their lives?

Characters and ideas
previous/next comment

179/191	Setting
183/190	Structure
179/188	Elizabeth-Jane
182/187	Henchard
186/189	Henchard
174/189	Character
179/191	Lucetta
186/200	Elizabeth-Jane
188/200	Character
187/191	Henchard
185/193	Structure
184/195	Setting
188/192	Lucetta
189/195	Henchard
191/193	Lucetta
162/281	Susan

193 'You probably are . . .'
Lucetta reveals that her motives for offering Elizabeth-Jane a position in her household are to give Henchard an excuse for coming to see her. Lucetta's plan to use Elizabeth-Jane in this way has echoes of Susan's plan to use Henchard's ignorance of Elizabeth-Jane's real father in order to get her into Henchard's home. Both plans do not work out quite so well as their originators had hoped.

171/194   Deception
190/197   Structure
192/194   Lucetta

194 It could not . . .
Hardy makes a biblical allusion to describe Lucetta's avoidance of the French language in order to protect the secrets of her past. The continued attempts by main characters to deceive and live a lie has far-reaching effects.

193/196   Lucetta
193/204   Deception

195 They sat in adjoining . . .
The view of the market place from the window of High-Place Hall is a further example of the narrative device of framing a scene. Note the many details which are described and commented on, and which build for us a picture of the central activities which occupy the businessmen of Casterbridge. Within that overall picture Farfrae and Henchard meet, but it is Henchard who declines to respond to Farfrae's unspoken invitation to resume their friendship.

191/203   Setting
182/200   Farfrae
191/199   Henchard

196 The days came . . .
Note the calculated way in which Lucetta assesses the prospect of marriage to Henchard. She is concerned with the regulation of her social position, not with love.

194/197   Lucetta

197 'Then where you are . . .'
Lucetta discovers Henchard's coolness towards Elizabeth-Jane and realizes that High-Place Hall is the one place he will avoid. Driven by Henchard's non-appearance to write yet another letter to him, Lucetta then arranges herself on a chair in a totally artificial and affected pose – a pose she suddenly abandons in favour of hiding behind the window curtains when she hears a visitor arriving. Why do you think she showed this sudden timidity? Note how easily she is upset: it prepares us for a more traumatic event later in the story.

193/198   Structure
196/201   Lucetta

198 She could hear . . .
Suspense is created when Lucetta, having hidden behind a curtain, reveals herself and discovers that her visitor is not Henchard as she had expected.

197/199   Structure

Chapter 23

199 'But I'm very . . .'
Farfrae comes to High-Place Hall to see Elizabeth-Jane, having been granted permission by Henchard. Ironically, it is Lucetta that he meets and the two are immediately attracted to one another. Note how the delay in his response to Henchard's note leads to this new situation. There would have

198/203   Structure
195/205   Henchard

seemed to be no good reason why he virtually ignored Elizabeth-Jane when he passed her by just after receiving the note.

200 Farfrae's sudden entry . . .

When Farfrae received the note from Henchard giving him permission to court Elizabeth-Jane he took no notice of it. Only subsequently did he decide to call on her. What are his reasons for showing an interest in her and what do they tell us about his character?

189/202	Character
188/206	Elizabeth-Jane
195/202	Farfrae

201 'Ay! Maybe you'll . . .'

Lucetta's declaration that she is lonely ignores the companionship of Elizabeth-Jane. Notice how Farfrae is suddenly driven to confide in her the details of his business successes of the last season.

177/251	Loneliness
197/202	Lucetta

202 'They do to me . . .'

Farfrae and Lucetta are attracted to one another because they are both shallow, calculating and over-sentimental. Do you agree with this statement? Can you relate incidents, for both characters, which would support such views, or others which would contradict them?

200/203	Character
201/204	Lucetta
200/204	Farfrae

203 The fair without . . .

Framed by the window, the view of the 'hiring fair' provides us with an interesting situation to watch. Note how the auctioning of one's services to the highest bidder and which, in this case, is likely to result in the separation of the young man and his sweetheart, has overtones of the incident many years ago at Weydon-Priors – but with a very different outcome. It also provides an opportunity for Farfrae to capture Lucetta's admiration.

195/207	Setting
199/214	Structure
202/220	Character

204 As he went . . .

The pressing needs of business come before this new relationship. Note how Lucetta warns him against gossip which may be directed at her reputation. It is ironic that her fears on this score will be fulfilled in such a dramatic manner later in the story.

202/206	Lucette
202/217	Farfrae
194/206	Deception

205 Three minutes later . . .

Yet again, Henchard arrives on the scene just too late to retrieve a situation which might have altered his future. Is he doomed by Fate to always take the wrong path, or is he getting the just rewards of a man who is too wrapped up in his own perception of what is right and just, and unable to see others' equally valid points of view?

199/206	Henchard

206 Elizabeth as a watch-dog . . .

Lucetta plans to let Elizabeth-Jane stay in order to keep Henchard away. Does everyone use and manipulate Elizabeth-Jane to suit their own purposes? Was Susan the only character who had her welfare at heart? Certainly Lucetta and Henchard allow their own plans and prejudices to come before any consideration of Elizabeth-Jane's welfare, but what of Farfrae? Does he actually 'use' her in any way for his own gain?

204/212	Deception
204/208	Lucetta
200/210	Elizabeth-Jane
205/209	Henchard

Chapter 24

	Characters and ideas previous/*next* comment

207 It was the . . .
The novel is set in the years immediately preceding the repeal of the Corn Laws. The changing face of agriculture is shown by the arrival of the horse drill in Casterbridge, where it causes much sensation.

203/208   Setting

208 Elizabeth-Jane's bonnet . . .
Lucetta appeared to be the 'only appropriate possessor of the new machine' because only she rivalled it in colour. In what way are Lucetta's dress and the new machine linked, apart from colour? Note the sensation that the machine causes.

207/209   Setting
206/211   Lucetta

209 'Yes,' Henchard replied; . . .
Do you think that Henchard ridicules the new machine because it represents the new order and he resents change? If so, how do you explain the admiration he showed for Farfrae's new methods in managing his own corn trade?

208/210   Setting
206/215   Henchard

210 'Then the romance of . . .'
Elizabeth-Jane's reaction to the new horse drill shows that she accepts the inevitability of change, but regrets the passing of the old ways, which were often more romantic and picturesque.

209/219   Setting
206/211   Elizabeth-Jane

211 'Yes.' And having . . .
What does Elizabeth-Jane's fixation with being respectable say about the life she has led so far? Note the irony of her comments about 'shadows'. Which of the main characters in this novel does not have a 'shadow'?

208/213   Lucetta
210/213   Elizabeth-Jane

212 'Yes,' said Lucetta . . .
Can you see any parallel between this conversation and the one that Henchard had with Farfrae about his past life?

206/272   Deception

213 There was something . . .
It is interesting to note how Lucetta seems to place so much reliance on Elizabeth-Jane's opinions – much as Henchard did on Farfrae's at the start of their relationship.

211/215   Lucetta
211/214   Elizabeth-Jane

Chapter 25

214 The next phase . . .
In this chapter Elizabeth-Jane becomes more and more identified with the role of narrator and it is through her eye that we see much of the action. She is possessed by a 'seer's spirit' which enables her to see the developing relationship of Lucetta and Farfrae, and to see through Lucetta's story.

203/234   Structure
213/219   Elizabeth-Jane

215 He crossed the room . . .
Note how possessive Henchard had felt towards Lucetta – 'as almost his property'. Is this how he felt, or at least acted towards Susan, and to some

213/216   Lucetta
209/216   Henchard

extent Elizabeth-Jane? Was there also a hint of this possessiveness in his relationship with Farfrae?

216 'Not at all!' . . .
Is Henchard capable of doing anything right? He has visited Lucetta in an attempt to further his cause with her, yet ends up arguing and, in her eyes, insulting her!

215/218	Lucetta
215/217	Henchard

217 A yellow flood . . .
Even nature seems to side with Farfrae. Note how Henchard again misses the moment that would reveal all to him.

139/226	Nature
204/219	Farfrae
216/219	Henchard

218 He had hardly . . .
Lucetta has come to Casterbridge in order to escape from her past. Why is there an ironic twist to her refusal to be a slave to the past?

169/233	Fate
181/240	Irony
216/219	Lucetta

219 Elizabeth-Jane, surveying the . . .
How do the views of Henchard and Farfrae on love and marriage differ from those of Lucetta and Elizabeth-Jane? That they both seem unaware of the effect of their actions on Elizabeth-Jane seems strange and possibly says a lot about their characters.

210/225	Setting
218/222	Lucetta
214/220	Elizabeth-Jane
217/221	Farfrae
217/221	Henchard

220 She had learnt . . .
Elizabeth-Jane now realizes the identity of both the men in Lucetta's story. She accepts the loss of Farfrae with resignation and grieves for her father, not understanding why he continues to neglect her.

203/221	Character
219/227	Elizabeth-Jane

Chapter 26

221 'Do you remember,' . . .
How ironic is this short conversation between the two men? Henchard, so wrapped up in his own thoughts and aspirations failed at his last meeting with Lucetta to see whom she now desired. His questioning of Farfrae deepens that irony, for Henchard does not know that Farfrae is the reason for Lucetta declining to marry him. Farfrae, deeply engrossed in reading Lucetta's letter, fails to make the connection between the woman Henchard is talking about and Lucetta. Is it that all the characters, with one or two notable exceptions, are so bound up in their own selfish desires and plans that they fail to see events happening under their own noses which will frustrate their plans? Could you call Elizabeth-Jane's desire to be respectable, selfish? Does this desire prevent her from taking a more spirited part in the pursuit of her own happiness?

220/222	Character
219/222	Farfrae
219/222	Henchard

222 'More bread-and-butter?'
One of the most humorous scenes in the novel is the one in which Lucetta and her two suitors take tea together. Humour emphasizes the tragedy of

219/236	Lucetta
221/223	Henchard

the situation as well as providing some light-hearted relief from the intensity of the encounter. However, is Elizabeth-Jane's comment 'How ridiculous of all three of them!' an apt comment on their stupidity and selfishness?

221/229	Character
221/228	Farfrae

223 But he was disturbed.
The mingling of business rivalry with rivalry in love is the major factor in persuading Henchard that he needs to do something quite drastic about Farfrae. His decision to call for Jopp is most misguided and, ironically, will not lead to the downfall of Farfrae but to the death of the woman Henchard loves, Lucetta.

222/224	Henchard
86/224	Joshua Jopp

224 'Indeed! Very good.'
The selection of Jopp as his corn manager shows very little good sense on Henchard's part. Note also the fact that Jopp was apparently in Jersey at the same time as Henchard. Will this have any significance for future events?

223/228	Henchard
223/230	Joshua Jopp

225 'Now,' said Henchard, . . .
The Corn Laws of 1815 and 1828 gave protection from foreign competition to the home corn trade. Consequently, prices depended on the home harvest to a large extent: the prospect of a bad harvest would force prices up and the promise of a good one would lower prices.

219/228	Setting

226 'I sometimes think', . . .
The income of the farming community was entirely dependent on the wheat crop, which in turn depended on the weather. In an agricultural town like Casterbridge the weather was central to every man's thoughts, taking on a god-like status.

217/228	Nature

227 Elizabeth-Jane heard by . . .
This assessment of Jopp as the wrong man for the job shows a degree of perception on her part. Elizabeth-Jane's tackling of Henchard on the subject shows some of the spirit which seemed to be there at times when she first appeared in the story.

220/238	Elizabeth-Jane

228 In a lonely hamlet . . .
Mr Fall, the weather prophet, makes a comfortable living by predicting the weather, although no one will admit to believing in his forecasts. How does the visit to the weather prophet contrast the business attitudes of Henchard and Farfrae?

226/243	Nature
225/232	Setting
224/229	Henchard
222/234	Farfrae

229 'Forecast the weather?'
Henchard's visit to the weather prophet confirms the traditional views which underpin Henchard's approach to his business. Five other farmers had already been to see the weather prophet on the same errand, and basically Henchard was no different from them. At a time of crisis at the start of the story he went to church and vowed to change—he had control over the success or otherwise of that vow. At this new time of crisis he goes to a very dubious source for advice, and he will have no control over the outcome.

228/230	Henchard
222/237	Character

230 Coming down the . . .

Note how Henchard always manages to fault others for mistakes and happenings which he set in motion. 'Act in haste, repent at leisure' is a very old truism. Henchard certainly does the former, but the latter rarely seems to play a part in his actions. His first thought seems always to be directed at finding a scapegoat.

231 'You shall be sorry . . .'

The dismissal of Jopp is a serious error of judgment on Henchard's part. Jopp had no reason to like Farfrae, having lost his job as manager to him, and Farfrae's success is the cause of Jopp losing the same job again. However, he has as many reasons to hate Henchard: the abrupt dismissal by Henchard when he first applied for the job as corn manager, and this second dismissal in circumstances that were hardly fair to him, leave him nursing a grievance against both Henchard and Farfrae.

Chapter 27

232 From that day . . .

The inability of Henchard to judge the right moment to do or say things has yet again led to a setback. He is driven to considering whether some power is working against him, and, coming so soon after his visit to the weather prophet, his wondering about a 'waxen image' points to the superstitions that lurk at the back of his mind.

233 'I wonder,' he . . .

Despite the disaster that Henchard has suffered, and the prospering of his rival, Farfrae, Henchard is unable to conceive that Farfrae had an evil hand in that disaster. There seems to be an almost perverse contrariness in the mind of Henchard with regard to the dealings he has with Farfrae, Lucetta and Elizabeth-Jane. At this point, when you would expect him to rail against Farfrae, he just descends into a 'moody depression'. Does he, perhaps, consider that it is not man, but Fate which contends against him?

234 Instead of considering . . .

The fight between the two waggoners foreshadows the fight between Henchard and Farfrae. Is there also something symbolic in the overturning of Henchard's hay in front of Elizabeth-Jane and Lucetta? An event will shortly bring the whole of his world tumbling down at his feet, just as his hay now lies.

235 Nearly the whole town . . .

The integration of the urban and farming communities of Casterbridge is demonstrated by the efforts of the populace who work on into the night to rescue the harvest.

236 'You are convinced, . . .

What request does Lucetta make to Farfrae when he proposes to her and what are her reasons for making it? Overheard conversations feature on a number of occasions. Like letters, they enable aspects of the action to progress and develop.

237 This unluckily aroused . . .

Henchard, feeling that he is about to lose the last 'thing' available to him, Lucetta, forces her to promise to marry him by threatening to reveal her past. He can show no mercy now that he knows Lucetta to be in love with Farfrae. It is ironic that Lucetta, who so quickly resorts to letter-writing in pursuing her desires, is to have her dearest wish frustrated by those same letters – or so it seems.

236/238	Lucetta
234/238	Henchard
229/240	Character

238 'Don't be a no'thern . . .'

Henchard required a witness to Lucetta's response, presumably to ensure the fulfilment of the verbal contract. However, in calling for Elizabeth-Jane to witness the harshness of his actions and the obvious reluctance of Lucetta to marry him, he prepares the ground for her final rejection of him.

237/239	Lucetta
227/246	Elizabeth-Jane
237/240	Henchard

239 Elizabeth-Jane continued . . .

The accusation that 'You have many secrets from me' touches on one of the key reasons why so many of the characters' plans fail to succeed. Every character in the novel is affected by the secrets and the resulting deceits that they or others practise.

238/243	Lucetta

Chapter 28

240 Henchard as a Justice . . .

It would seem ironic that Henchard's 'rough and ready perceptions' which were so well suited to the simple cases he dealt with in court, did not ease the complications of his own life. Has he dealt justly with Farfrae, Susan, Lucetta, Elizabeth-Jane, Jopp or Whittle? In answering this question you ought to have a clear idea of what you mean by justice, and be able to point to incidents which support your arguments. Do also be aware of Henchard's point of view in these matters and the pressures he is under.

218/246	Irony
237/243	Character
238/241	Henchard

241 'Twenty years ago . . .'

Note how fate intervenes with the reappearance of the old furmity woman and the fact that Henchard is standing in for Dr Chalkfield as a magistrate.

240/242	Henchard
234/255	Fate

242 'No – 'tis true.'

This will not be the furmity woman's last appearance in the novel, but for Henchard it is the catastrophe to which events and fate seem to have been building up. The one secret which set all the events in motion and which he has been able to conceal is now made public in the most spectacular way. Almost fatalistically he makes no attempt to deny the furmity woman's allegations, but merely acknowledges their truth. This is the decisive moment of the novel for Henchard. With the exposure of his last secret his fall is guaranteed.

236/246	Structure
241/246	Henchard

243 A gradual misery . . .
What do you think is the cause of Lucetta's misery? Note her mood which is reflected by the places she visits before deciding to go away to Port Bredy.

Chapter 29

244 At this hour . . .
How does Lucetta's mood on her walk along the Port Bredy road suggest some development in her relationship with Farfrae, thereby creating suspense?

245 They looked round . . .
Do you think the episode of the bull is an example of Hardy contriving events in order to hold the interest of his serial readers? If not, what relevance does it have to the story? The violence with which Henchard controlled the bull to some extent suggests the lack of finesse with which he approaches personal relationships, and how he is attempting to bully his way into the position of Lucetta's husband – but is this a sufficient justification for the episode? What it does do is bring Henchard and Lucetta together so that he can be informed of the failure of his plan to marry her.

246 'I'll run back,' . . .
It is ironic that in rescuing the two women from the bull Henchard takes great care over the hysterical Lucetta, who is already the wife of his rival, while ignoring Elizabeth-Jane who will be his only comfort in the future.

247 'No, no!' said . . .
Henchard attempts to use his relationship with Lucetta in order to demonstrate his credit-worthiness. Note how this reflects the incident with Susan at the start of the novel. He used Susan to acquire money and 'lost' her as a result. His attempt to use Lucetta to gain credit will be followed very swiftly by the knowledge that he has lost her as well!

248 The notes of . . .
The town band celebrates the marriage of Lucetta and Farfrae. What other event introduced the town band to us and how did it contrast with these celebrations of Farfrae's victory in love and business?

249 'A pensioner of . . .'
Henchard's pride prevents him from accepting any financial assistance from the wife of his rival.

Chapter 30

250 At the last . . .
Farfrae sends Lucetta home from Port Bredy ahead of himself because he has business to attend to and he feels that Lucetta is in the best position to break

the news to the 'inmates' of her house. To what extent does Farfrae's attitude to his bride coincide with what we know of his character?

251 Lucetta uttered a . . .

Is Elizabeth-Jane worse or better off for not acting as Lucetta suggests? Certainly it keeps her from the knowledge of Henchard's actions those many years before. Of all the characters, perhaps Elizabeth-Jane is the most used and abused. Yet she gives freely of her love and affection. Is there a slight parallel here with Abel Whittle?

201/259	Loneliness
247/274	Lucetta
246/252	Elizabeth-Jane

252 Any suspicion of . . .

Why does Elizabeth-Jane condemn Lucetta for marrying Farfrae and not Henchard? To what extent do you think she is justified in her belief in Lucetta's impropriety?

247/253	Setting
251/253	Elizabeth-Jane

253 'You–have–married . . .'

Hardy makes a biblical reference to illustrate Elizabeth-Jane's total condemnation of Lucetta. From pleasure that the thought of Lucetta's marriage to her father had brought, to the distress over the actual marriage to Farfrae, Elizabeth-Jane's world is in something of a turmoil.

252/259	Setting
252/254	Elizabeth-Jane

254 Here she sat . . .

Alone at last, Elizabeth-Jane is thrown onto her own resources. Could she reasonably have stayed in the same house as Lucetta and Farfrae, especially given her fierce pursuit of respectability? Note how, almost casually, Lucetta accepted her leaving the house. She seems to have no concern at all for Elizabeth-Jane's immediate future – only the problems she faces as a result of marrying Farfrae without telling him the whole truth about her background.

253/266	Elizabeth-Jane

Chapter 31

255 New events combined . . .

Events beyond Henchard's control play a part in his downfall, when one of his men misrepresents the quality of some corn, blackening Henchard's name.

249/257	Henchard
241/270	Fate

256 Small as the . . .

Note the author's assessment of the state of Henchard's affairs. There will shortly be another 'fillip downward' when the period of his vow of abstinence runs out.

248/258	Structure

257 'Well,' said the senior . . .

Henchard acts honestly at the bankruptcy hearing and especially when he sells his watch to pay off the poorest of his creditors – could you regard it, though, as merely an act of defiance at a world to which he wants to owe nothing at all?

250/258	Character
255/260	Henchard

258 When everything was . . .
The story began with an auction whereby Henchard acquired the determination to succeed in his life. That success culminates in another auction where all the fruits of his determination are disposed. Has he anything left, morally, spiritually or physically?

256/265 Structure
257/264 Character

259 She wrote to . . .
In contrast to the large house in Corn Street, Henchard moves to Jopp's cottage near the Priory Mill. The gloomy atmosphere of this part of Casterbridge emphasizes his despair.

251/263 Loneliness
253/261 Setting

260 Abel Whittle was . . .
Abel Whittle contrasts life in the corn stores before and after Farfrae's takeover. How does this contrast reveal differences in the characters of Henchard and Farfrae?

134/342 Abel Whittle
250/261 Farfrae
257/261 Henchard

261 The intelligence was . . .
The triumph of the new, scientific farming methods over the old ways is evident from the use of scales and steelyards for measuring, where guesswork had formerly been the rule. The change reflects some of the differences between Henchard and Farfrae, and their differences in turn reflect the wider changes that were taking place in society about that time.

259/263 Setting
260/262 Henchard
260/264 Farfrae

Chapter 32

262 'Gone into my . . .'
Jopp takes pleasure in telling Henchard about Farfrae's purchase of his house and furniture. Note how Jopp's presence always seems to threaten trouble.

231/287 Joshua Jopp
261/263 Henchard

263 The low land grew . . .
Note how the description of the sky and landscape surrounding the stone bridge conveys Henchard's mood of loneliness, gloom and despair.

259/306 Loneliness
262/264 Henchard
261/267 Setting

264 'No; but what I . . .'
Farfrae offers Henchard accommodation and shows him great kindness. Why does Henchard refuse this apparently generous offer? Does it appear that Farfrae has discussed this matter with Lucetta? It may be a kindness to Henchard, but what would it have been to Lucetta? There is a strange contradiction in Farfrae, from the sentimentality he sometimes shows in his relationship with Henchard, to the lack of it in his dealings with business, Lucetta and Elizabeth-Jane. Perhaps he sees the two ladies as part of 'business' arrangements?

258/266 Character
263/265 Henchard
261/265 Farfrae

265 They walked into . . .
Note the almost cruel parody which this meeting between the two men is of their first meeting – even to the offer of a meal.

258/269 Structure
264/267 Henchard
264/269 Farfrae

266 However, the ice . . .
Elizabeth-Jane hears of Henchard's illness and goes to visit him. What effect does her kindness have on him?

264/267	Character
254/270	Elizabeth-Jane

267 'I have worked . . .'
Why do you think that Henchard continues to wear his suit rather than the traditional dress of the hay-trusser?

263/285	Setting
266/268	Character
265/268	Henchard

268 Elizabeth-Jane sat at . . .
The release of Henchard from his vow sets the seal on his downfall. There remains but one thing for him to lose, the respect and love of Elizabeth-Jane, and he takes a sure path to accomplish that event.

267/269	Henchard
267/271	Character

Chapter 33

269 Now the Three Mariners . . .
Note how this scene is reminiscent of that occasion when Farfrae sang at the Three Mariners inn. However, there is none of that goodwill and respect to be found here. Henchard's violent temper is still evident when he forces the choir to sing a psalm which curses Farfrae, but also laments his own position.

268/270	Henchard
265/272	Farfrae
265/278	Structure

270 'Thank ye, thank . . .'
How is Henchard's observation that when he was rich he did not need what he could have, and now he is poor he cannot have what he needs, similar to an observation made by Elizabeth-Jane in chapter 25?

255/277	Fate
266/304	Elizabeth-Jane
269/271	Henchard

271 'Ah, my boys, you've . . .'
Is this gesture of his, breaking the poker across his knees, the origin of his decision to physically attack his rival?

268/273	Character
270/272	Henchard

272 For two or three . . .
At this meeting we are reminded that despite all the shocks of recent, past events, there are still great matters of secrecy and deception between these four people – matters which have yet to take their toll on the persons involved.

212/304	Deception
269/273	Farfrae
271/274	Henchard

273 Henchard did not . . .
Farfrae avoids doing anything which might seem like triumphing over a fallen rival. To what extent do you think Farfrae is acting sincerely?

271/274	Character
272/275	Farfrae

274 'Will you,' said . . .
What aspects of Lucetta's character are we reminded of by the note she sends to Henchard reprimanding him for the sarcastic way in which he spoke to her at the corn store?

273/275	Character
251/281	Lucetta
272/276	Henchard

Chapter 34

275 She asked him . . .
Although Farfrae dismisses Elizabeth-Jane's fears that Henchard means him harm, his calculating nature makes him reflect on what she has told him, and he begins to take the threat seriously. Note also the lack of feeling and respect he shows her speaking as he does with 'the cheeriness of a superior'.

274/276	Character
273/276	Farfrae

276 'Is that so—. . .'
In the midst of an act of kindness Farfrae learns of Henchard's bitterness. Consider carefully Farfrae's comment 'what harm have I done him that he should try to wrong me?'. Has he done Henchard any harm, knowingly? Should he have been more perceptive in his relations with Henchard, Lucetta and Elizabeth-Jane? Or is there nothing in his life but success in business and the trappings that go with it? If this is the case consider how we should judge him as a man.

275/280	Character
275/277	Farfrae
274/278	Henchard

277 Farfrae seemed seriously . . .
Lucetta's plan to leave Casterbridge is upset by the news of Dr Chalkfield's death. Farfrae is offered the position of mayor. Farfrae often invokes providence, but do you think fate really rules his life, or something much more tangible like ambition? Certainly fate seems to be interfering with Lucetta's scheme to remove her husband from the possible discovery of her past relationship with Henchard!

270/286	Fate
276/278	Farfrae

278 On the very . . .
Farfrae has completely replaced Henchard—as corn-factor, as Lucetta's husband and now as Mayor of Casterbridge. As Farfrae has risen, so Henchard has fallen.

269/282	Structure
277/297	Farfrae
276/280	Henchard

279 Henchard returned to . . .
Note this use of grim, ironic humour to make the reading of Lucetta's letters to Farfrae more dramatic and to create suspense.

246/307	Irony

280 He opened a third . . .
Henchard is unable to reveal the name of the person who wrote the letters he has read to Farfrae. What does this tell us about his character? How does Henchard later explain his act of reading the letters? Do you find it strange that Farfrae should not guess at what has happened? Should he not at least wonder why Henchard is flaunting the letters in his face?

276/283	Character
278/286	Henchard

Chapter 35

281 The usual time for . . .
Note the irony of this reference to 'spirits from the grave'. Secrets have a nasty way of catching up with one—you will recall how Susan was referred to as 'The Ghost' by the town boys.

274/282	Lucetta
192/285	Susan

282 She went back . . .
Note how this, and previous demonstrations of Lucetta's tendency to become hysterical when she is under pressure, prepare us for events which occur later in the novel.

278/285	Structure
281/283	Lucetta

283 This was sufficient.
Lucetta finds it impossible to tell Farfrae the truth. She wants to escape from her past instead of accepting responsibility for it, because she believes that he would see her relationship with Henchard as 'her fault rather than her misfortune'. Do you think she is right in her assessment of her husband's attitude?

280/284   Character
282/284   Lucetta

284 To herself she . . .
Note how carefully Lucetta plans her appearance before Henchard. Does this reveal something about her character, or show us the desperate straits to which the deception of her husband has driven her?

283/298   Character
283/285   Lucetta

285 Nor could any . . .
Events come full circle with the return of Henchard to the Ring to meet the other woman in his life. As Susan wanted something for Elizabeth-Jane, so now Lucetta asks for something from Henchard. Why is it likely that perhaps our sympathies would lie more with Susan than with Lucetta?

267/289   Setting
284/287   Lucetta
282/287   Structure
281/0   Susan

286 Henchard silently looked . . .
Henchard envies Lucetta's love for Farfrae even though he can now see her weaknesses. Note how Henchard's attempts to achieve a loving relationship always seem to be snatched away from him just as he is about to grasp the opportunity. Even when he thinks he has the power to force the event to happen, something prevents it.

277/301   Fate
280/288   Henchard

Chapter 36

287 'But your can . . .'
The presence of Jopp threatens trouble once again. Lucetta's refusal to speak favourably of him to Farfrae makes him long for revenge. Do you think the references that Jopp has made to Jersey, both to Henchard and Lucetta, pose a threat or are merely 'red herrings' introduced by the author to create some suspense?

285/288   Structure
262/288   Joshua Jopp
285/304   Lucetta

288 He handed a package . . .
Henchard wants to free Lucetta from her past indiscretions, so he agrees to return her letters and asks Jopp to deliver them. In parcelling up the letters he fails to seal them properly; where else did the author use this device of poorly sealed letters to set a sequence of events in motion?

287/291   Structure
286/295   Henchard
287/0   Joshua Jopp

289 Mixen Lane was . . .
The description of Mixen Lane as the home of those in distress, debt and every kind of trouble, completes our view of Casterbridge society.

285/290   Setting

290 Yet amid so . . .
The changing face of rural Wessex is illustrated by reference to the families of decayed villages whose legal rights had expired, thus depriving them of homes which had been theirs for generations.

289/294   Setting

291 'Yes – 'tis not . . .'
The furmity woman makes her last appearance in the novel and again sets events in motion. It is she who asks Jopp what is in the parcel he carries.

288/292   Structure

292 The plank was . . .
The arrival of a stranger in Casterbridge by such a strange route creates suspense. Do we have any clues as to the identity of the stranger? Is it apt that he should walk over a plank to enter Casterbridge?

291/293   Structure

293 'Ah, I remember . . .'
The irony involved in the stranger's action of paying out money is not yet apparent, but it will become so!

292/294   Structure

Chapter 37

294 Such was the state . . .
Is there an irony of contrast in the two preparations that are taking place: one for the skimmington ride, and the other for the ride of a royal personage through the town? Note how both events represent a different stage in the history and development of Casterbridge, and in the fortunes of Lucetta and Henchard. One reflects the past history of the town, the other its growing importance in a fast-changing world. One will lead to the death of Lucetta and the other to the final degradation and eventual death of Henchard.

290/295   Setting
293/301   Structure

295 It had been . . .
To what extent is Henchard's plan to welcome the royal personage an ironic contrast between the old and new ways of rural life?

294/296   Setting
288/296   Henchard

296 From the background . . .
There is something pathetic yet defiant in the appearance of Henchard dressed in 'weather-beaten garments of bygone years'. It is in stark contrast to the rest of Casterbridge. It also emphasizes the fate of those who are unable to come to terms with change.

295/326   Setting
295/298   Henchard

297 In the crowd . . .
The triumph of Farfrae and Lucetta is seen in contrast to the views of the townsfolk. Christopher Coney remarks that as a man of money, Farfrae has lost some of the charm he had when he first came to Casterbridge as a 'light-hearted, penniless youth'. Farfrae's happiness now seems complete, as does Lucetta's. There would appear to be nothing that could now upset their settled life.

160/302   Rustics
278/299   Farfrae

Chapter 38

298 After the collision . . .
Henchard overhears Lucetta deny that he ever assisted Farfrae or that he was anything more than a common workman. What effect does this have upon Henchard?

284/299   Character
296/299   Henchard

299 'Wait a bit . . .'
Although Henchard hates Farfrae and has decided to kill him, he wants to make the fight fair, so he binds one of his arms to his side. Note the catalogue of 'insults' which Henchard recites. Could they in any way justify an attempt to kill Farfrae, whether or not in a fair fight?

297/302   Farfrae
298/300   Henchard
298/306   Character

300 Henchard took his . . .
Note the tragic depths to which Henchard has descended. Especially so when the author refers to this previously manly figure as crouching in an attitude more appropriate to a woman.

299/306   Henchard

301 He became possessed . . .
The overheard conversation will bring Henchard and Farfrae together again, but ironically, the circumstances which led Henchard to overhear the conversation will prevent Farfrae from believing him.

286/305   Fate
294/303   Structure

Chapter 39

302 When he was just . . .
Farfrae's popularity with his men is evident from their attempt to get him out of the way by sending him an anonymous letter.

297/325   Rustics
299/310   Farfrae

303 It was about . . .
The suspense of the skimmington ride is heightened by the way it is contrasted with Lucetta's feeling of security, believing that her incriminating letters have been destroyed.

301/309   Structure

304 Lucetta started to . . .
The accurate descriptions of the clothing worn leaves Lucetta in no doubt about who the figures represent, and although Elizabeth-Jane tries to protect her friend from the spectacle of the skimmington ride, Lucetta forces her way onto the balcony to witness the public destruction of her last secret.

272/309   Deception
287/305   Lucetta
270/317   Elizabeth-Jane

305 The doctor arrived . . .
Lucetta's attempts to hide the truth and escape her past only lead her to incriminate herself further. In the end, the past which she refused to be enslaved by kills her.

301/309   Fate
304/0   Lucetta

Chapter 40

306 But, alas! for Henchard . . .
Henchard is filled with remorse at the thought of his attack upon Farfrae. He resolves to find him and inform him of Lucetta's illness. However, those at the house and then Farfrae distrust him. How does this rejection and loss of self-respect affect Henchard?

300/307   Henchard
263/322   Loneliness
299/308   Character

307 The gig and its . . .
Henchard's attempt to persuade Farfrae to return is a failure and the irony of the situation is stressed by a biblical allusion to Job, who, when brought to justice for his crimes cursed 'the day in which he was born, the night during which he was conceived, and his whole existence'.

279/311   Irony
306/308   Henchard

308 Henchard regarded the . . .
In his despair, Henchard sees hope in Elizabeth-Jane and resolves to love her despite the fact that she is not his daughter. However, note the condition: 'if only she would continue to love him'. He still seems unprepared to give, without looking for a return on his 'investment'.

304/311   Elizabeth-Jane
307/310   Henchard
306/310   Character

309 'He seemed a . . .'
Our suspicions that the stranger to Casterbridge might be Newson are strengthened further when Jopp tells Henchard that a sea-captain of some sort had called. Note the cruelty of fate. Just when Henchard has resolved to try and love Elizabeth-Jane, a threat from the past emerges. Note also how his resolve to love Elizabeth-Jane did not include making a clean breast of the past and the knowledge he had regarding her true parentage. Perhaps if he had done so and not decided to continue the deceit he might have retained her love.

305/311   Fate
304/312   Deception
303/344   Structure
63/313   Newson

310 The divergence to . . .
To what extent do you think that Farfrae's distracted state is also due to his shame at rejecting Henchard? How do we know that despite the fight the two men still care for one another?

302/319   Farfrae
308/311   Henchard
308/315   Character

Chapter 41

311 To please him, . . .
Elizabeth-Jane muses on the appalling unexpectedness of Lucetta's death amid such promise of happiness. It is perhaps fittingly ironic that she should think this, comfortably settled on a couch in her 'father's' lodgings with him looking to her comfort, especially given the event about to happen.

309/312   Fate
310/312   Henchard
308/317   Elizabeth-Jane
307/0   Irony

312 Meanwhile her stepfather . . .
Unable to learn from his experiences Henchard dreams of a future 'lit by her filial presence', when he knows full well that 'filial presence' is a lie of his and Susan's construction. From our past experiences of the events in the novel we must surely recognize that there is no way that fate will allow such happiness.

309/314   Deception
311/314   Henchard
311/316   Fate

313 'My name is Henchard.'
Our suspicions are confirmed. The stranger in Casterbridge reveals himself as Newson. His reappearance in the novel may seem incredible, almost as much as his later, swift disappearance. However, he is the only one who can impart to Elizabeth-Jane the knowledge of her true parentage, something we can assume that Henchard will never do.

309/329   Newson

314 'Dead likewise,' said . . .
These 'mad lies like a child, in pure mockery of consequences' will be the final undoing of Henchard. Amazed at the lie he has told Newson, characteristically, he immediately regrets his impulsiveness.

312/315	Deception
312/315	Henchard

315 This probability threw . . .
Henchard feels ashamed at what he has done, but his fear of losing Elizabeth-Jane prevents him from accepting responsibility for his actions and so he proceeds to build a web of lies to protect himself.

314/316	Henchard
314/317	Deception
310/317	Character

316 In place of them . . .
Henchard is unable to 'summon music' to sooth him in these dark times. Note how again Henchard's mood is reflected in the sombre nature of the natural setting.

243/340	Nature
315/317	Henchard
312/318	Fate

317 'I thought you seemed . . .'
Elizabeth-Jane's 'natural insight' enables her to see Henchard's desperation and she offers to come and live with him; ironically it does not enable her to guess the secret that Henchard has kept from her.

315/320	Character
316/318	Henchard
311/321	Elizabeth-Jane
315/327	Deception

318 'Ah – to be sure – . . .'
Henchard refrains from committing suicide when he sees the effigy of himself floating in Ten Hatches. He wonders why he is the only one left alive, unable to see that his turn will come.

317/319	Henchard
316/331	Fate

Chapter 42

319 Henchard and himself . . .
Note how Farfrae, despite all the troubles which Henchard has caused, shows a lasting regard for the man by assisting in the purchase of a small business for him.

310/320	Farfrae
318/321	Henchard

320 But as a memory, . . .
Farfrae's grief for Lucetta is diminished by his knowledge of her past which would have interfered with their future happiness. What does this suggest about Farfrae's character?

317/322	Character
319/335	Farfrae

321 By the end of . . .
This relationship, idyllic though it is, has in it the seeds of disaster. Henchard senses that Elizabeth-Jane is civil rather than affectionate to him.

317/323	Elizabeth-Jane
319/322	Henchard

322 Henchard went away, . . .
Henchard's suspicions of the growing relationship between Elizabeth-Jane and Farfrae make him afraid of losing her. He cannot accept that her marriage to Farfrae would be for her good and his own. Is he incapable of learning from experience?

320/324	Character
321/324	Henchard
306/330	Loneliness

	Characters and ideas *previous/next* comment

323 Elizabeth admitted that . . .
With the shock of recent events fading from memory, Elizabeth-Jane's walks in the direction of the sea ought to give us a premonition of things to come.

321/325 Elizabeth-Jane

324 Henchard vowed that . . .
Henchard vows that he will not interfere in the relationship of Farfrae and Elizabeth-Jane. What other examples of Henchard's restraint can you give? Whatever the faults of the man, there do seem to be certain depths of conduct to which he refuses to sink. There is a continual struggle in the novel between the two major aspects of his character. There is his 'rough benignity' on the one hand and his 'temperament that would have no pity for weakness' on the other.

322/327 Character
322/327 Henchard

Chapter 43

325 Perhaps the only . . .
The locals of the Three Mariners voice their approval of the match between Farfrae and Elizabeth-Jane. The once cynical Christopher Coney shows his admiration for Elizabeth-Jane. In the passions and conflicts which centre on Henchard we perhaps tend to overlook the trials and tribulations through which Elizabeth-Jane goes. Yet her most testing time is yet to come.

302/342 Rustics
323/338 Elizabeth-Jane

326 Elizabeth, as has been . . .
The description of the prehistoric fort of Mai Dun and of the old Roman Via gives a perspective of time and history to the Budmouth road on which Farfrae and Elizabeth-Jane meet. It is here whilst spying on the progress of the romance that Henchard sees Newson again.

296/328 Setting

327 Then he would tell her . . .
Elizabeth-Jane receives a message that someone wishes to meet her at Farfrae's house. She asks Henchard's permission, which he gives, showing that he has finally admitted the truth to himself. What do you think would have been the outcome if, at this stage and having nothing to lose, he were to tell Elizabeth-Jane the truth that he had for so long concealed? It is perhaps indicative of the state to which he had been brought that he had no stomach for the scene that such an admission would have caused. Perhaps if he had been able to admit the truth, the future would have been different – or would it?

324/329 Character
324/328 Henchard
317/338 Deception

328 He went secretly . . .
Henchard exchanges his shabby, genteel suit for the clothes of his trade. The way he leaves Casterbridge is contrasted with his arrival some twenty-five years earlier. Do you think he leaves a wiser man?

326/332 Setting
327/330 Henchard

329 'Ah, I thought I . . .'
Newson treats Henchard's lie as a joke. What does this tell us about his character? What do you think is the main function of the character of Newson in the novel? Note, however, how Elizabeth-Jane receives the

327/331 Character
313/337 Newson

news. Henchard was certainly correct in his judgment that there would be no place for him in Casterbridge when the news was broken to his 'daughter'.

Chapter 44

330 Meanwhile the man . . .
Henchard is a rejected and lonely man. He sleeps out in the open and feels no want of food, and thus we are partly prepared for the events to come. The autumn sun reminds us of events which now seem so very long ago. The few pathetic reminders he keeps of a girl who was no kin to him say a great deal about how low his spirits have sunk.

328/331 Henchard
322/334 Loneliness

331 The renowned hill . . .
Henchard returns to the site of the Weydon fair which reminds him of the crimes of his past. He recognizes his failures, and particularly the way his ambition had destroyed his life, and his loves. He finds himself back in exactly the same position that he was in a quarter of a century before, except that he is much wiser. Ironically, however, he no longer has the will and zest for life that would enable him to profit from his past mistakes.

318/342 Fate
329/333 Character
330/333 Henchard

332 'Yes – I've come . . .'
Note how the changing rural scene is emphasized by the road waggoner who expresses his fear of the competition of the railways. The railway came to Dorchester in 1847.

328/0 Setting

333 'But yes, John – . . .'
There was another wedding which took place in the late autumn which should kindle memories for Henchard. Can you remember whose it was? Henchard decides to return to Casterbridge remembering Elizabeth-Jane's regret that he would miss the wedding. Consider his decision to try and obtain forgiveness. Is this yet another example of Henchard's inability to attempt to do the right thing at the right time?

331/335 Character
331/334 Henchard

334 Henchard did not . . .
Henchard's loneliness is symbolized by the lonely figure on the broad, white highway which he portrays. This image of people travelling along lonely dusty roads frequently appears in the novel.

333/336 Henchard
330/336 Loneliness

335 Henchard dusted his . . .
The voice of Farfrae can be heard emanating from the wedding festivities. Note the sarcastic observation made about Farfrae loving his country so much that he never revisited it. It is worth considering whether or not you feel that his love for music and song is only a surface emotion and that beneath the words is no real strength of feeling. Look at the other occasions when he sings, what are the circumstances that lead him to sing?

333/338 Character
320/341 Farfrae

336 The door of the . . .
We have seen so many of this novel's incidents framed through doorways and windows. Invariably the framing adds something to the interpretation of the scene. Note how the view of the wedding party through the doorway emphasizes Henchard's feeling of loneliness and exclusion.

334/337	Henchard
334/340	Loneliness

337 By degrees Henchard . . .
The view of Newson's happy face is the final depressing vision for Henchard; all of his hopes are dashed – he 'stood like a dark ruin . . . his own soul upthrown'.

336/339	Henchard
329/0	Newson

338 She flushed up . . .
Elizabeth-Jane's sense of moral indignation at Henchard's deception makes her reject him. The theme of deception that has run so strongly throughout the entire novel has reached its concluding moment and Henchard reaps the final reward of the events which he set in motion so many years ago.

335/339	Character
325/345	Elizabeth-Jane
327/0	Deception

339 Henchard's lips half . . .
What is it in Henchard's character that prevents him from explaining his actions and attempting to gain the forgiveness he desires?

338/341	Character
337/340	Henchard

Chapter 45

340 In exploring her . . .
The bird image, which was first seen at the beginning of the novel, returns in the shape of the dead, caged goldfinch. To what extent do you think that the goldfinch which died of starvation symbolizes Henchard rejected and starved of love? Note how the discovery softens Elizabeth-Jane's attitude, so that ironically, Henchard gains, too late, what he had so earnestly desired.

339/343	Henchard
336/0	Loneliness
316/0	Nature

341 When her husband . . .
What final proof do we have of Farfrae's shallow and calculating nature?

339/344	Character
335/345	Farfrae

342 'Yes, ma'am, he's gone! . . .'
Note how the tragedy of Henchard's death is emphasized by the pathos of Abel Whittle's loyalty in repaying Henchard for the kindness he showed to Abel's mother.

325/0	Rustics
331/0	Fate
260/0	Abel Whittle

343 'Yes, ma'am, he's gone! . . .'
The caged bird dies because it was physically prevented from eating. Henchard dies, having lost the will to live. His 'cage' was the loss of all he had striven and lived for.

340/344	Henchard

344 'That Elizabeth-Jane Farfrae . . .'
Of the many notes and letters that have featured in the story, the last one comes from the pen of Henchard. It includes no attempt to deceive nor endeavours to promote self-interest. Henchard's will asks for no recognition or reward, but bitterly speaks of a soul broken and a life wasted.

341/346   Character
309/0   Structure
343/0   Henchard

345 What Henchard had . . .
Note the author's comment that Elizabeth-Jane recognized the force of Henchard's last wish and the fact that she would not ignore it to achieve her own peace of mind. Note also the remark about her husband's 'large-heartedness'. Does this also comment on the motives behind all those other occasions when Farfrae demonstrated 'large-heartedness'?

338/346   Elizabeth-Jane
341/0   Farfrae

346 Her teaching had . . .
Elizabeth-Jane has, by her moderation and practicality, enabled herself to live a happier life. She has learnt through painful experience to accept the indifference of fate and to make the best of limited opportunities. Although her marriage to Farfrae has brought her much to be thankful for, she is aware of the inevitability of change and the uncertainty of the future.

345/0   Elizabeth-Jane
344/0   Character

Characters in the novel

This is a very brief overview of each character. You should use it as a starting point for your own studies of characterization. For each of the aspects of character mentioned you should look in your text for evidence to support or contradict the views expressed here, and indeed, your own views as well.

Know the incidents and conversations which will support and enlarge upon your knowledge of each character. You will find it helpful to select a character and follow the commentary, referring always to the text to read and digest the context of the comment.

Michael Henchard

As the title of the novel makes clear, Henchard is the tragic hero of the story. He is a heavy-framed man of great physical power and energy. When we meet him at the beginning of the novel he shows a haughty indifference to everyone around him. The drunken sale of his wife shows that he can be cruel, impulsive and bad-tempered. Henchard's reactions to his deeds when he wakes the next day show he is remorseful and yet too full of shame to make a loud hue and cry, though he searches for his wife and child for several months. We soon realize that he is a lonely man who has substituted ambition for love.

Although he is often brutal in his behaviour towards Elizabeth-Jane and Lucetta, he has a strong sense of responsibility which he shows in his desire to make amends to Susan. He is a man who cannot control his passions. We see Henchard's fall in contrast to the rise of Farfrae, but unlike the emotionally shallow Farfrae, Henchard learns the need to express his love and he comes to respect Elizabeth-Jane as a woman, even though she is not his daughter.

Not only does Henchard have to learn to accept responsibility for his past actions but also for events beyond his control. He is a victim of fate and his superstitious nature often makes him believe that a sinister power is working against him. No sooner does he learn to love Elizabeth-Jane than his love is threatened by the return of Newson. His deception results in Elizabeth-Jane's rejection and he goes away to die totally alone and defeated.

Donald Farfrae

Farfrae is an important character in the novel, but his main function is to contrast the character of Henchard. When he arrives in Casterbridge he is the young, ambitious stranger who has left his native land to make his fortune in much the same way as Henchard must have done nineteen years earlier. However, we soon see his character is very much the opposite of Henchard's. He is calculating, moderate and sensible and easily responds and adapts to the new, scientific farming methods. Although he sings with great pathos which endears him to the hearts of the townsfolk, there seems to be no depth to his emotions. He sacrifices love to ambition in not proposing to Elizabeth-Jane after he has fallen out with Henchard. It is not until after the death of Lucetta that we really see the flaws in Farfrae's character. Although he is fair and generous in his dealings he fails to feel anything passionately and is more concerned about not making 'a hole in a sovereign'.

Susan Newson/Henchard

Susan appears at the beginning of the novel to be a meek even simple-minded woman, but the vehemence with which she throws her wedding ring at Henchard after he has sold her to Newson suggests there is more to her character than meets the eye. Both Henchard and Newson regard her as a simple home-spun woman, not at all shrewd or sharp, but she manages to keep Elizabeth-Jane's paternity a secret in order to ensure a comfortable future for her. She shows great cunning in bringing her daughter and Farfrae together. Her dedication to Elizabeth-Jane shows that she is affectionate and self-sacrificing.

Elizabeth-Jane

Elizabeth-Jane is important because, as her character develops, it is through her eyes that we see much of the action; she replaces the narrator as observer and commentator. She has been taught by poverty and the loss of her father to endure pain and hardship. Although her passage through life is often rough she endures loneliness and the frustration of her love with a quiet acceptance. She has a natural insight and innate kindness and even when she loses Farfrae to Lucetta, shows no jealousy. Her strong sense of duty and propriety, however, leads her to reject Henchard at the moment he most needs her love and forgiveness. The happiness and peace of mind she has found in her marriage to Farfrae is sobered by the bitterness expressed in Henchard's will. She is, at the end of the novel, a mature woman who makes the most of limited opportunities but remains aware of the persistent consequences of unforeseen circumstances.

Lucetta Templeman/Le Sueur

Lucetta is a woman whose past casts a shadow over her life. She is of French descent and comes from Jersey where she met and cared for Henchard during his illness. They fell in love and their relationship, being contrary to Victorian moral standards, caused a scandal. Her aunt dies leaving an inheritance which enables her to set herself up in style in Casterbridge.

Her character is shallow, over-sentimental and artful. She takes great care over her appearance and uses people for her own advantage. Lucetta has a habit of writing letters and, although she fears disclosure of her past, this habit only serves to incriminate her further. Despite having promised to marry Henchard, she refuses to be a slave to the past and secretly marries Farfrae in Port Bredy. Ironically, it is the past that kills her when her love letters to Henchard are used as the reason for the skimmington ride.

Richard Newson

The character of Richard Newson is not developed very much and his main function is to help the plot along. He is a kind man and a loving husband and father. His consideration for Susan's feelings when he knows her to be unhappy about their relationship makes him go away to sea so that she can go back to Henchard if she wishes. His trusting nature borders on the naïve and he forgives Henchard's lie, treating it as a practical joke. His joviality at the wedding festivities enables him to 'out-Farfrae Farfrae'. His love of the sea prevents him from staying long in Casterbridge even though it is the home of his daughter.

Joshua Jopp

Jopp is a very minor character, but his appearance always seems to signify trouble. In all fairness to Jopp he is a much-abused character. First, he arrives at the corn-factor's office to be told that the position of manager has already been filled. He is bitterly disappointed and this incident does not endear him to Henchard or Farfrae. Then, Jopp is hired as manager by Henchard to cut out Farfrae but, when the plan goes wrong, it is Jopp who is blamed and dismissed. Despite Henchard's dislike for Jopp he takes lodgings in his cottage. Jopps takes satisfaction in telling Henchard that Farfrae has moved into his old house and bought his furniture.

The final rebuff to Jopp is administered by Lucetta when he asks her to speak favourably of him to Farfrae. Armed with Lucetta's incriminating package he enjoys a partial revenge when their contents lead to the skimmington ride, but this ends tragically leaving Jopp plagued by anxiety. To a certain extent his inability to make a real and lasting success of anything he does, mirrors the frustrations that afflict Henchard.

Abel Whittle

Abel Whittle is really one of the rustics, but he does appear at crucial points in the novel. He is a foolish, simple-minded man of no education. Abel is very unreliable and cannot get out of bed in the morning. This brings about a clash between Farfrae and Henchard when the latter treats him harshly after he has failed to turn up for work on time. The second time we meet Whittle is much later in the novel when Farfrae has taken over Henchard's business. He comments that, though he has to work harder for less money, he is the richer man for having a peace of mind with Farfrae which he never had with Henchard. We meet Whittle at the end of the novel when he performs a simple act of kindness in caring for the dying Henchard, to repay him for his kindness to Abel's mother.

What happens
in each chapter

Chapter 1 A hay-trusser with his wife and child are approaching the village of Weydon-Priors on a late summer's evening. There is a fair in progress and they enter a tent for refreshment. The man takes his furmity laced with rum, and in a drunken state sells his wife and child by auction to a sailor for five guineas.

Chapter 2 When the young man awakes next morning he realizes what he has done and makes a hasty departure from the fairground. He goes into the first church he comes across and swears an oath that he, Michael Henchard, will avoid all strong liquors for twenty-one years. He searches everywhere for his wife and child, though not as vigorously as he might, finally learning that persons of their description have emigrated. He gives up his search and makes for the town of Casterbridge.

Chapter 3 Nineteen years later Susan Henchard and her daughter, Elizabeth-Jane, are approaching Weydon-Priors by the same road on fair day. Susan now calls herself Mrs Newson. The two women are mourning for the sailor, Richard Newson. They find the fair much smaller, but the furmity woman is still there, now fallen on hard times. Susan learns from the woman that Henchard was in Casterbridge twelve months after selling his wife.

Chapter 4 An outline of Susan's life with Newson, first in Canada and then in Falmouth, is given as a flashback. A friend of Susan's ridicules her belief that there is anything legally binding in her relationship with Newson. Shortly after, Newson is lost at sea. Susan sets out to try to find a better life for Elizabeth-Jane by searching for her husband. They arrive in Casterbridge where the people are angry with the corn-factor who has sold overgrown wheat, making the bread indigestible.

Chapter 5 Attracted by the music of the town band the two women proceed to the King's Arms where they observe Henchard as Mayor of Casterbridge and successful corn merchant. The loftiness of his social position causes Susan some discomfort. They notice, however, that Henchard drinks water though wine and rum are available.

Chapter 6 A young man, Farfrae, overhears the criticisms levelled at the corn-factor and sends a note to him. He then decides to lodge at the more modest Three Mariners inn. Susan and Elizabeth-Jane also decide to stay there. Later in the evening Henchard goes to see the young man at the inn.

Chapter 7 Elizabeth-Jane works in the Three Mariners to pay for the lodgings. Susan overhears Farfrae telling Henchard how to restore the grown wheat. The corn-factor is so grateful to the young man that he offers him a job as his manager. Farfrae declines because he has made up his mind to go to America. Before he leaves Henchard refuses a drink and explains that he swore an oath against strong liquor out of shame for a past deed.

Chapter 8 The Scotsman, Farfrae, joins the company of the Three Mariners and gives a recital of some of his native songs. Everyone is very impressed by the emotion he shows, particularly Elizabeth-Jane. Henchard, in the High Street outside the Three Mariners, also hears Farfrae's voice and is drawn to him.

Chapter 9 Next morning, Henchard accompanies Farfrae to the Bristol road. Susan sends Elizabeth-Jane to Henchard with a letter. When she arrives she finds Farfrae there instead of Henchard. We discover that the corn-factor has persuaded the young man to stay on in Casterbridge.

Chapter 10 Before Elizabeth-Jane can enter Henchard's office Joshua Jopp pushes in and announces himself as the new manager. He is disappointed to learn that the position has been filled. Elizabeth-Jane gives the message to Henchard who sends her back with a letter for Susan in which he encloses five guineas. He arranges to meet Susan at the Ring on the Budmouth road.

Chapter 11 An atmosphere of gloom is created by the Ring with its gruesome, historical associations. Henchard meets Susan and proposes a plan by which he can court and remarry her without revealing his past, either publicly or to Elizabeth-Jane.

Chapter 12 Returning from his meeting with Susan, Henchard invites Farfrae to supper and confides in him the story of his marriage and separation from Susan. He tells him of his plans to remarry her and of the complication posed by the woman in Jersey whom he has also offered to marry. He asks Farfrae to help him draft a letter explaining the circumstances which prevent him fulfilling his promise. He does not tell Farfrae that he sold his wife and daughter.

Chapter 13 Henchard hires a cottage for Susan and Elizabeth-Jane where he visits them frequently. After a few months he marries her and although it is not a joyous occasion the plan is almost complete. Henchard has fulfilled his three resolves, namely to make amends to Susan, provide a home for Elizabeth-Jane and to punish himself for his past actions.

Chapter 14 Susan and Elizabeth-Jane now live easier and more affluent lives. Elizabeth-Jane continues to dress modestly and doesn't draw attention to herself by spending a lot of money. Susan opposes the final part of Henchard's plan to adopt her daughter and change her name. Someone plays a trick on Farfrae and Elizabeth-Jane by arranging for them to meet in an empty granary.

Chapter 15 Elizabeth-Jane is admired in the town for her beauty and dress sense. A rift appears in the friendship of the two men when they quarrel over Henchard's harsh treatment of one of his workmen. Henchard comes out worse, finding he has lost some of the respect he had among the townsfolk. Their friendship continues, but Henchard often wishes that he had not confided the secrets of his life to Farfrae.

Chapter 16 On the occasion of a national holiday, both men organize separate festivities. Henchard's are very elaborate, in the open air and free of charge. Farfrae's are under cover and with a charge for admission. On the day, it rains heavily and Henchard's festivities are washed out. Farfrae's are very successful and the comments of the townsfolk goad Henchard into saying that his manager is about to leave him. Farfrae takes him at his word.

Chapter 17 After the festivities Farfrae walks Elizabeth-Jane home and almost proposes to her. When he leaves Henchard's employment, he sets up in business on his own, at first avoiding competition with him, but later having to engage in commercial combat in self-defence. Henchard forbids Farfrae to see his daughter.

Chapter 18 A letter arrives from Jersey. A young woman, Lucetta, writes to Henchard and asks him to return her old letters as she passes through Casterbridge. She fails to keep the appointment and Henchard is left with the packet of letters. Susan falls ill and writes a letter to her husband with the instruction that it should not be opened until Elizabeth-Jane's wedding day. Susan confesses to having written the notes which brought her daughter and Farfrae together at the granary. Susan dies.

Chapter 19 Henchard cannot resist telling Elizabeth-Jane what he thinks is the truth–that she is his daughter, not Newson's. While searching for some proof of this he comes across Susan's letter which he reads because it has been badly sealed. He discovers that his child died and that Elizabeth-Jane is in fact Newson's daughter. Henchard resolves not to tell Elizabeth-Jane and she accepts him as her father.

Chapter 20   Bitterly disappointed that she is not his daughter, Henchard finds fault in everything that Elizabeth-Jane does despite her attempts at self-improvement. While tending her mother's grave she meets a young woman who suggests that Elizabeth-Jane should come to live with her as her companion. Henchard is anxious to rid himself of Newson's daughter, so he writes to Farfrae to tell him that he no longer objects to him seeing Elizabeth-Jane.

Chapter 21   Elizabeth-Jane goes to look at High-Place Hall and nearly bumps into Henchard who is also showing interest in the place. She leaves her home in Corn Street to live with Lucetta Templeman. When Henchard realizes how Elizabeth-Jane has tried to improve herself he is greatly moved and asks her to stay on but his request comes ten minutes too late.

Chapter 22   Henchard's visit to High-Place Hall the previous evening is explained. Lucetta writes to him to say that she has moved to Casterbridge. He realizes the cause of his confusion to be the fact that Lucetta has taken her aunt's name of Templeman. Lucetta writes to Henchard again, but when he visits her she refuses to see him until the next day. The mayor is rather annoyed at this and puts off his visit for several days. Lucetta learns of the coldness between Elizabeth-Jane and Henchard and realizes that she will have to get rid of the girl. A visitor is shown in and Lucetta, thinking it is Henchard, hides behind a curtain.

Chapter 23   The visitor is Farfrae, who has come to see Elizabeth-Jane. Lucetta is immediately attracted to him. Farfrae saves two lovers from being parted by hiring the young man and his father. Farfrae leaves having forgotten the reason for his visit. Henchard arrives, but Lucetta refuses to see him, and now appreciates Elizabeth-Jane's presence as a means of keeping Henchard away.

Chapter 24   Lucetta and Elizabeth-Jane live for market days when they will catch a glimpse of Farfrae. One Saturday a new machine arrives in Casterbridge and the two women go to inspect it. When they encounter Farfrae, Elizabeth-Jane senses an attraction between him and Lucetta. Later, Lucetta relates a story to her (pretending that it is not herself) about a woman who was promised to one man but had since met another whom she preferred. Elizabeth-Jane refuses to judge the case, but realizes that the woman is Lucetta.

Chapter 25   Both Farfrae and Henchard call on Lucetta, but although the latter offers to marry her she puts off making a decision. Both men show total indifference to Elizabeth-Jane who suffers her rejection silently.

Chapter 26   Henchard suspects that it is Farfrae who is his rival in love and hires Joshua Jopp as his manager to cut Farfrae out by fair competition. Jopp is only too pleased to do this as he bears a grudge against Farfrae. Henchard goes to consult a weather prophet before he puts his plan into operation and is told that the harvest will be a wash out. He buys up as much grain as possible, hoping to sell it later at a profit. The weather looks as though it will be fine and Henchard is forced to sell at a loss for which he blames Jopp and dismisses him.

Chapter 27   No sooner does the harvest begin when the rain comes, proving the weather prophet right after all. Rivalry between Henchard and Farfrae grows and this is taken up by their men. Henchard follows Lucetta and Farfrae and overhears their conversation. He visits Lucetta later in the evening and by threatening to reveal their past relationship, forces her to promise to marry him. Elizabeth-Jane is called as a witness.

Chapter 28   By coincidence Henchard is presiding at the magistrates' court in place of Dr Chalkfield, the mayor. Here the furmity woman from Weydon-Fair is being tried and she discloses the story of how Henchard sold his wife and child. Lucetta hears of the story and is worried about the promise of the previous evening. She goes away for a few day's rest to Port Bredy.

Chapter 29   Lucetta is walking along the Port Bredy road when she meets Elizabeth-Jane. The two women are chased into a barn by a bull and it is Henchard who saves them and subdues the animal. Henchard takes the hysterical Lucetta home and learns that she has already married Farfrae in Port Bredy.

Chapter 30   Lucetta discloses her marriage to Elizabeth-Jane and asks her to stay on at High-Place Hall. Elizabeth-Jane is shocked at her impropriety and immediately takes lodgings on her own.

Chapter 31   Henchard's unfortunate business transactions lead him into bankruptcy, but at the hearing he acts fairly and even sells his gold watch to pay the poorest of his creditors. He goes to live in Jopp's cottage, giving orders that he wishes to see no one. Even Elizabeth-Jane is turned away. Farfrae takes over Henchard's business where he continues to be popular despite working the men harder and paying them less.

Chapter 32   Henchard spends much of his time standing on the two bridges with other unfortunates. Jopp tells him that Farfrae has moved into his old house and bought up his furniture. Farfrae is generous to Henchard, but the latter refuses assistance. Henchard falls ill and is comforted by Elizabeth-Jane who gives him some hope for the future. Farfrae gives him employment in his old trade, but on hearing that Farfrae is to be proposed as mayor Henchard becomes bitter and looks forward to the end of his vow of abstinence. .

Chapter 33   Henchard, now free from his oath, drinks in the Three Mariners. One Sunday he forces the choir to sing a psalm with harsh and threatening words, which he directs at Farfrae. Elizabeth-Jane takes him home, but his threats make her feel it is her duty to warn Farfrae. Henchard behaves sarcastically to Lucetta, who incriminates herself with yet another letter in which she asks him to refrain from speaking to her in such a way.

Chapter 34   Elizabeth-Jane warns Farfrae of Henchard's hatred towards him, but he dismisses her fears. However, when the information is confirmed by someone else he abandons a plan to set Henchard up in a seedman's shop. Lucetta asks Henchard to return her old letters and he remembers they are in his old safe in the house now occupied by Farfrae and Lucetta. He goes there that evening fully intending to disclose the contents to Farfrae, but although he reads some of the letters out aloud, he hasn't the heart to reveal the name of the sender.

Chapter 35   Lucetta has overheard Henchard reading out the letters. She writes to him again and pleads with him to return them. They arrange to meet at the Ring and the surroundings remind Henchard of his mistreatment of Susan and he promises to return the letters.

Chapter 36   As Lucetta returns home from her meeting with Henchard she meets Jopp who asks her to recommend him as manager to Farfrae. She dismisses him. Henchard asks Jopp to deliver the package of letters to Lucetta, but on his way there he calls at the Peter's Finger. The package is opened and the contents disclosed to the assembled company. They arrange a skimmington ride to punish Lucetta for her impropriety. The letters are repacked and delivered to Lucetta who immediately burns them. Meanwhile a stranger arrives in Casterbridge.

Chapter 37   Henchard asks the council if he can join them in welcoming a visiting royal personage, but is refused. On the day he appears in his shabby clothes waving a flag and is roughly ordered away by Farfrae. Lucetta is goaded by the talk of some of the other women. The skimmington ride has been planned for that night.

Chapter 38   Henchard wants revenge over Farfrae and asks for a meeting in the granary. He binds one of his arms because he is the stronger man and when Farfrae arrives starts to fight him. Henchard overpowers Farfrae but cannot bring himself to throw the young man out of the granary. Henchard is ashamed of what he has done. Farfrae goes off to Weatherbury, summoned by an anonymous letter.

Chapter 39   The anonymous letter had come from Longways and some of Farfrae's other men, in an attempt to lure him away from the scene of the skimmington ride. Lucetta hears the approach of the procession and although Elizabeth-Jane appears and tries to prevent her from seeing it, she becomes hysterical and insists on looking out. When she sees the effigies she has what would appear to be an epileptic fit. The procession disappears without trace.

Chapter 40   On seeing the skimmington ride, Henchard goes to find Elizabeth-Jane and follows her to Farfrae's house. He learns of Lucetta's illness and of the doctor's request for Farfrae to come immediately. Realizing that Farfrae had changed his plans, Henchard goes to try to find him, but Farfrae refuses to trust him. When Farfrae finally returns he is distressed at his mistrust of Henchard, as well as at his wife's condition. Lucetta dies after revealing her secret. Henchard returns home to discover that a sea captain has called to visit him.

Chapter 41   Elizabeth-Jane visits Henchard to inform him of Lucetta's death. He sees that she is tired and encourages her to rest while he makes the breakfast. Newson, the sailor, calls and enquires about Elizabeth-Jane and Henchard tells him she is dead. The naïve Newson accepts his word and leaves Casterbridge. Henchard immediately regrets his lie, but filled with fear of losing Elizabeth-Jane's love, resolves to keep the truth from her. Elizabeth-Jane offers to come and live with him.

Chapter 42   Newson does not return and Henchard lives with Elizabeth-Jane running a small seedman's shop bought for him by the council. Farfrae realizes that the revelation of Lucetta's secret would have damaged their relationship and now turns his attentions towards Elizabeth-Jane. Henchard is jealous and fears losing her but vows not to interfere in their courtship.

Chapter 43   Henchard sees Newson return and, taking up the clothes and trade of a hay-trusser, leaves Casterbridge in much the same way as he had arrived, a quarter of a century before. Elizabeth-Jane receives a note from a stranger who wants to meet her at Farfrae's house. Going there she is reunited with her father. She learns how Henchard has prevented her father from seeing her until now and turns against him.

Chapter 44   Henchard returns to Weydon-Priors and the scene of his earlier crimes. He obtains work as a hay-trusser and realizes he could start again, but he does not have the will to do so. He learns of the approach of Elizabeth-Jane's wedding day and decides to make one last attempt to seek her love and forgiveness. He returns to Casterbridge and arrives at the wedding festivities. Elizabeth-Jane rejects him and he takes his leave, before she can collect her thoughts, unable to begin to explain his actions.

Chapter 45   After the wedding the caged goldfinch which Henchard had brought as a present is found dead from starvation. After several weeks Elizabeth-Jane discovers that it was Henchard who brought it and resolves to find him. They search everywhere and are about to give up when they see Abel Whittle. Abel informs them how he followed Henchard from Casterbridge and looked after him until his death. He leaves a will pinned to his bed requesting that his memory be obliterated.

Coursework and preparing for the examination

If you wish to gain a certificate in English literature then there is no substitute for studying the text/s on which you are to be examined. If you cannot be bothered to do that, then neither this guide nor any other will be of use to you.

Here we give advice on studying the text, writing a good essay, producing coursework, and sitting the examination. However, if you meet problems you should ask your teacher for help.

Studying the text

No, not just read – study. You must read your text at least twice. Do not dismiss it if you find a first reading difficult or uninteresting. Approach the text with an open mind and you will often find a second reading more enjoyable. When you become a more experienced reader enjoyment usually follows from a close study of the text, when you begin to appreciate both what the author is saying and the skill with which it is said.

Having read the text, you must now study it. We restrict our remarks here to novels and plays, though much of what is said can also be applied to poetry.

1 You will know in full detail all the major incidents in your text, **why**, **where** and **when** they happen, **who** is involved, **what** leads up to them and what follows.

2 You must show that you have an **understanding of the story**, the **characters**, and the **main ideas** which the author is exploring.

3 In a play you must know what happens in each act, and more specifically the organization of the scene structure – how one follows from and builds upon another. Dialogue in both plays and novels is crucial. You must have a detailed knowledge of the major dialogues and soliloquies and the part they play in the development of plot, and the development and drawing of character.

4 When you write about a novel you will not normally be expected to quote or to refer to specific lines but references to incidents and characters must be given, and they must be accurate and specific.

5 In writing about a play you will be expected both to paraphrase dialogue and quote specific lines, always provided, of course, that they are actually contributing something to your essay!

To gain full marks in coursework and/or in an examination you will also be expected to show your own reaction to, and appreciation of, the text studied. The teacher or examiner always welcomes those essays which demonstrate the student's own thoughtful response to the text. Indeed, questions often specify such a requirement, so do participate in those classroom discussions, the debates, class dramatizations of all or selected parts of your text, and the many other activities which enable a class to share and grow in their understanding and feeling for literature.

Making notes

A half-hearted reading of your text, or watching the 'film of the book' will not give you the necessary knowledge to meet the above demands.

As you study the text jot down sequences of events; quotations of note; which events precede and follow the part you are studying; the characters involved; what the part being studied contributes to the plot and your understanding of character and ideas.

Write single words, phrases and short sentences which can be quickly reviewed and which will help you to gain a clear picture of the incident being studied. Make your notes neat and orderly, with headings to indicate chapter, scene, page, incident, character, etc, so that you can quickly find the relevant notes or part of the text when revising.

Writing the essay

Good essays are like good books, in miniature; they are thought about, planned, logically structured, paragraphed, have a clearly defined pattern and development of thought, and are presented clearly – and with neat writing! All of this will be to no avail if the tools you use, i.e. words, and the skill with which you put them together to form your sentences and paragraphs are severely limited.

How good is your general and literary vocabulary? Do you understand and can you make appropriate use of such terms as 'soliloquy', 'character', 'plot', 'mood', 'dramatically effective', 'comedy', 'allusion', 'humour', 'imagery', 'irony', 'paradox', 'anti-climax', 'tragedy'? These are all words which examiners have commented on as being misunderstood by students.

Do you understand 'metaphor', 'simile', 'alliteration'? Can you say what their effect is on you, the reader, and how they enable the author to express himself more effectively than by the use of a different literary device? If you cannot, you are employing your time ineffectively by using them.

You are writing an English literature essay and your writing should be literate and appropriate. Slang, colloquialisms and careless use of words are not tolerated in such essays.

Essays for coursework

The exact number of essays you will have to produce and their length will vary; it depends upon the requirements of the examination board whose course you are following, and whether you will be judged solely on coursework or on a mixture of coursework and examination.

As a guide, however your course is structured, you will be required to provide a folder containing at least ten essays, and from that folder approximately five will be selected for moderation purposes. Of those essays, one will normally have been done in class-time under conditions similar to those of an examination. The essays must cover the complete range of course requirements and be the unaided work of the student. One board specifies that these pieces of continuous writing should be a minimum of 400 words long, and another, a minimum of 500 words long. Ensure that you know what is required for your course, and do not aim for the minimum amount – write a full essay then prune it down if necessary.

Do take care over the presentation of your final folder of coursework. There are many devices on the market which will enable you to bind your work neatly, and in such a way that you can easily insert new pieces. Include a 'Contents' page and a front and back cover to keep your work clean. Ring binders are unsuitable items to hand in for **final** assessment purposes as they are much too bulky.

What sort of coursework essays will you be set? All boards lay down criteria similar to the following for the range of student response to literature that the coursework must cover.

Work must demonstrate that the student:

1 shows an understanding not only of surface meaning but also of a deeper awareness of themes and attitudes;

2 recognizes and appreciates ways in which authors use language;

3 recognizes and appreciates ways in which writers achieve their effects, particularly in how the work is structured and in its characterization;

4 can write imaginatively in exploring and developing ideas so as to communicate a sensitive and informed personal response to what is read.

Much of what is said in the section **Writing essays in an examination** (below) is relevant here, but for coursework essays you have the advantage of plenty of time to prepare your work–so take advantage of it.

There is no substitute for arguing, discussing and talking about a question on a particular text or theme. Your teacher should give you plenty of opportunity for this in the classroom. Listening to what others say about a subject often opens up for you new ways to look at and respond to it. The same can be said for reading about a topic. Be careful not to copy down slavishly what others say and write. Jot down notes then go away and think about what you have heard, read and written. Make more notes of your own and then start to clarify your own thoughts, feelings and emotions on the subject about which you are writing. Most students make the mistake of doing their coursework essays in a rush—you have time so use it.

Take a great deal of care in planning your work. From all your notes, write a rough draft and then start the task of really perfecting it.

1 Look at your arrangement of paragraphs, is there a logical development of thought or argument? Do the paragraphs need rearranging in order? Does the first or last sentence of any paragraph need redrafting in order to provide a sensible link with the preceding or next paragraph?

2 Look at the pattern of sentences within each paragraph. Are your thoughts and ideas clearly developed and expressed? Have you used any quotations, paraphrases, or references to incidents to support your opinions and ideas? Are those references relevant and apt, or just 'padding'?

3 Look at the words you have used. Try to avoid repeating words in close proximity one to another. Are the words you have used to comment on the text being studied the most appropriate and effective, or just the first ones you thought of?

4 Check your spelling and punctuation.

5 Now write a final draft, the quality of which should reflect the above considerations.

Writing essays in an examination
Read the question. Identify the key words and phrases. Write them down, and as they are dealt with in your essay plan, tick them off.

Plan your essay. Spend about five minutes jotting down ideas; organize your thoughts and ideas into a logical and developing order–a structure is essential to the production of a good essay. Remember, brief, essential notes only!

Write your essay
How long should it be? There is no magic length. What you must do is answer the question set, fully and sensitively in the time allowed. You will probably have about forty minutes to answer an essay question, and within that time you should produce an essay between roughly 350 and 500 words in length. Very short answers will not do justice to the question, very long answers will probably contain much irrelevant information and waste time that should be spent on the next answer.

How much quotation? Use only that which is apt and contributes to the clarity and quality of your answer. No examiner will be impressed by 'padding'.

What will the examiners be looking for in an essay?
1 An answer to the question set, and not a prepared answer to another, albeit slightly similar question done in class.

2 A well-planned, logically structured and paragraphed essay with a beginning, middle and end.

3 Accurate references to plot, character, theme, as required by the question.

4 Appropriate, brief, and if needed, frequent quotation and references to support and demonstrate the comments that you are making in your essay.

5 Evidence that reading the text has prompted in you a personal response to it, as well as some judgment and appreciation of its literary merit.

How do you prepare to do this?
1 During your course you should write between three to five essays on each text.

2 Make good use of class discussion etc, as mentioned in a previous paragraph on page 75.

3 Try to see a live performance of a play. It may help to see a film of a play or book, though be aware that directors sometimes leave out episodes, change their order, or worse, add episodes that are not in the original – so be very careful. In the end, there is no substitute for **reading and studying** the text!

Try the following exercises without referring to any notes or text.

1 Pick a character from your text.

2 Make a list of his/her qualities – both positive and negative ones, or aspects that you cannot quite define. Jot down single words to describe each quality. If you do not know the word you want, use a thesaurus, but use it in conjunction with a dictionary and make sure you are fully aware of the meaning of each word you use.

3 Write a short sentence which identifies one or more places in the text where you think each quality is demonstrated.

4 Jot down any brief quotation, paraphrase of conversation or outline of an incident which shows that quality.

5 Organize the list. Identify groupings which contrast the positive and negative aspects of character.

6 Write a description of that character which makes full use of the material you have just prepared.

7 What do you think of the character you have just described? How has he/she reacted to and coped with the pressures of the other characters, incidents, and the setting of the story? Has he/she changed in any way? In no more than 100 words, including 'evidence' taken from the text, write a balanced assessment of the character, and draw some conclusions.

You should be able to do the above without notes, and without the text, unless you are to take an examination which allows the use of plain texts. In plain text examinations you are allowed to take in a copy of your text. It must be without notes, either your own or the publisher's. The intention is to enable you to consult a text in the examination so as to confirm memory of detail, thus enabling a candidate to quote and refer more accurately in order to illustrate his/her views that more effectively. Examiners will expect a high standard of accurate reference, quotation and comment in a plain text examination.

Sitting the examination

You will have typically between two and five essays to write and you will have roughly 40 minutes, on average, to write each essay.

On each book you have studied, you should have a choice of doing at least one out of two or three essay titles set.

1 **Before sitting the exam**, make sure you are completely clear in your mind that you know exactly how many questions you must answer, which sections of the paper you must tackle, and how many questions you may, or must, attempt on any one book or in any one section of the paper. If you are not sure, ask your teacher.

2 **Always read the instructions** given at the top of your examination paper. They are

there to help you. Take your time, and try to relax – panicking will not help.

3 **Be very clear about timing, and organizing your time.**

(a) Know how long the examination is.
(b) Know how many questions you must do.
(c) Divide (b) into (a) to work out how long you may spend on each question. (Bear in mind that some questions may attract more marks, and should therefore take proportionately more time.)
(d) Keep an eye on the time, and do not spend more than you have allowed for any one question.
(e) If you have spare time at the end you can come back to a question and do more work on it.
(f) Do not be afraid to jot down notes as an aid to memory, but do cross them out carefully after use – a single line will do!

4 **Do not rush the decision** as to which question you are going to answer on a particular text.

(a) Study each question carefully.
(b) Be absolutely sure what each one is asking for.
(c) Make your decision as to which you will answer.

5 **Having decided which question** you will attempt:

(a) jot down the key points of the actual question – use single words or short phrases;
(b) think about how you are going to arrange your answer. Five minutes here, with some notes jotted down will pay dividends later;
(c) write your essay, and keep an eye on the time!

6 **Adopt the same approach** for all questions. Do write answers for the maximum number of questions you are told to attempt. One left out will lose its proportion of the total marks. Remember also, you will never be awarded extra marks, over and above those already allocated, if you write an extra long essay on a particular question.

7 **Do not waste time** on the following:

(a) an extra question – you will get no marks for it;
(b) worrying about how much anyone else is writing, they can't help you!
(c) relaxing at the end with time to spare – you do not have any. Work up to the very moment the invigilator tells you to stop writing. Check and recheck your work, including spelling and punctuation. Every single mark you gain helps, and that last mark might tip the balance between success and failure – the line has to be drawn somewhere.

8 **Help the examiner.**

(a) Do not use red or green pen or pencil on your paper. Examiners usually annotate your script in red and green, and if you use the same colours it will cause unnecessary confusion.
(b) Leave some space between each answer or section of an answer. This could also help you if you remember something you wish to add to your answer when you are checking it.
(c) Number your answers as instructed. If it is question 3 you are doing, do not label it 'C'.
(d) Write neatly. It will help you to communicate effectively with the examiner who is trying to read your script.

Glossary of literary terms

Mere knowledge of the words in this list or other specialist words used when studying literature is not sufficient. You must know when to use a particular term, and be able to describe what it contributes to that part of the work which is being discussed.

For example, merely to label something as being a metaphor does not help an examiner or teacher to assess your response to the work being studied. You must go on to analyse what the literary device contributes to the work. Why did the author use a metaphor at all? Why not some other literary device? What extra sense of feeling or meaning does the metaphor convey to the reader? How effective is it in supporting the author's intention? What was the author's intention, as far as you can judge, in using that metaphor?

Whenever you use a particular literary term you must do so with a purpose and that purpose usually involves an explanation and expansion upon its use. Occasionally you will simply use a literary term 'in passing', as, for example, when you refer to the 'narrator' of a story as opposed to the 'author' – they are not always the same! So please be sure that you understand both the meaning and purpose of each literary term you employ.

This list includes only those words which we feel will assist in helping you to understand the major concepts in play and novel construction. It makes no attempt to be comprehensive. These are the concepts which examiners frequently comment upon as being inadequately grasped by many students. Your teacher will no doubt expand upon this list and introduce you to other literary devices and words within the context of the particular work/s you are studying – the most useful place to experience and explore them and their uses.

Plot This is the plan or story of a play or novel. Just as a body has a skeleton to hold it together, so the plot forms the 'bare bones' of the work of literature in play or novel form. It is however, much more than this. It is arranged in time, so one of the things which encourages us to continue reading is to see what happens next. It deals with causality, that is how one event or incident causes another. It has a sequence, so that in general, we move from the beginning through to the end.

Structure The arrangement and interrelationship of parts in a play or novel are obviously bound up with the plot. An examination of how the author has structured his work will lead us to consider the function of, say, the 43 letters which are such an important part of *Pride and Prejudice*. We would consider the arrangement of the time-sequence in *Wuthering Heights* with its 'flashbacks' and their association with the different narrators of the story. In a play we would look at the scene divisions and how different events are placed in a relationship so as to produce a particular effect; where soliloquies occur so as to inform the audience of a character's innermost emotions and feelings. Do be aware that great works of fiction are not just simply thrown together by their authors. We study a work in detail, admiring its parts and the intricacies of its structure. The reason for a work's greatness has to do with the genius of its author and the care of its construction. Ultimately, though, we do well to remember that it is the work as a whole that we have to judge, not just the parts which make up that whole.

Narrator   A narrator tells or relates a story. In *Wuthering Heights* various characters take on the task of narrating the events of the story: Cathy, Heathcliff, etc, as well as being, at other times, central characters taking their part in the story. Sometimes the author will be there, as it were, in person, relating and explaining events. The method adopted in telling the story relates very closely to style and structure.

Style   The manner in which something is expressed or performed, considered as separate from its intrinsic content or meaning. It might well be that a lyrical, almost poetical style will be used, for example concentrating on the beauties and contrasts of the natural world as a foil to the narration of the story and creating emotions in the reader which serve to heighten reactions to the events being played out on the page. It might be that the author uses a terse, almost staccato approach to the conveyance of his story. There is no simple route to grasping the variations of style which are to be found between different authors or indeed within one novel. The surest way to appreciate this difference is to read widely and thoughtfully and to analyse and appreciate the various strategies which an author uses to command our attention.

Character   A person represented in a play or story. However, the word also refers to the combination of traits and qualities distinguishing the individual nature of a person or thing. Thus, a characteristic is one such distinguishing quality: in *Pride and Prejudice*, the pride and prejudices of various characters are central to the novel, and these characteristics which are associated with Mr Darcy, Elizabeth, and Lady Catherine in that novel, enable us to begin assessing how a character is reacting to the surrounding events and people. Equally, the lack of a particular trait or characteristic can also tell us much about a character.

Character development   In *Pride and Prejudice*, the extent to which Darcy's pride, or Elizabeth's prejudice is altered, the recognition by those characters of such change, and the events of the novel which bring about the changes are central to any exploration of how a character develops, for better or worse.

Irony   This is normally taken to be the humorous or mildly sarcastic use of words to imply the opposite of what they say. It also refers to situations and events and thus you will come across references such as prophetic, tragic, and dramatic irony.

Dramatic irony   This occurs when the implications of a situation or speech are understood by the audience but not by all or some of the characters in the play or novel. We also class as ironic words spoken innocently but which a later event proves either to have been mistaken or to have prophesied that event. When we read in the play *Macbeth*:

> *Macbeth*
> Tonight we hold a solemn supper, sir,
> And I'll request your presence.

> *Banquo*
> Let your highness
> Command upon me, to the which my duties
> Are with a most indissoluble tie
> Forever knit.

we, as the audience, will shortly have revealed to us the irony of Macbeth's words. He does not expect Banquo to attend the supper as he plans to have Banquo murdered before the supper occurs. However, what Macbeth does not know is the prophetic irony of Banquo's response. His 'duties. . . a most indissoluble tie' will be fulfilled by his appearance at the supper as a ghost – something Macbeth certainly did not forsee or welcome, and which Banquo most certainly did not have in mind!

Tragedy   This is usually applied to a play in which the main character, usually a person of importance and outstanding personal qualities, falls to disaster through the combination of personal failing and circumstances with which he cannot deal. Such tragic happenings may also be central to a novel. In *The Mayor of Casterbridge*, flaws in Henchard's character are partly responsible for his downfall and eventual death.

In Shakespeare's plays, *Macbeth* and *Othello*, the tragic heroes from which the two plays take their names, are both highly respected and honoured men who have proven

80	*Glossary of literary terms*

their outstanding personal qualities. Macbeth, driven on by his ambition and that of his very determined wife, kills his king. It leads to civil war in his country, to his own eventual downfall and death, and to his wife's suicide. Othello, driven to an insane jealousy by the cunning of his lieutenant, Iago, murders his own innocent wife and commits suicide.

Satire   Where topical issues, folly or evil are held up to scorn by means of ridicule and irony – the satire may be subtle or openly abusive.

In *Animal Farm*, George Orwell used the rebellion of the animals against their oppressive owner to satirize the excesses of the Russian revolution at the beginning of the 20th century. It would be a mistake, however, to see the satire as applicable only to that event. There is a much wider application of that satire to political and social happenings both before and since the Russian revolution and in all parts of the world.

Images   An image is a mental representation or picture. One that constantly recurs in *Macbeth* is clothing, sometimes through double meanings of words: 'he seems rapt withal', 'Why do you dress me in borrowed robes?', 'look how our partner's rapt', 'Like our strange garments, cleave not to their mould', 'Whiles I stood rapt in the wonder of it', 'which would be worn now in their newest gloss', 'Was the hope drunk Wherein you dressed yourself?', 'Lest our old robes sit easier than our new.', 'like a giant's robe upon a dwarfish thief'. All these images serve to highlight and comment upon aspects of Macbeth's behaviour and character. In Act 5, Macbeth the loyal soldier who was so honoured by his king at the start of the play, struggles to regain some small shred of his self-respect. Three times he calls to Seyton for his armour, and finally moves toward his destiny with the words 'Blow wind, come wrack, At least we'll die with harness on our back' – his own armour, not the borrowed robes of a king he murdered.

Do remember that knowing a list of images is not sufficient. You must be able to interpret them and comment upon the contribution they make to the story being told.

Theme   A unifying idea, image or motif, repeated or developed throughout a work.

In *Pride and Prejudice*, a major theme is marriage. During the course of the novel we are shown various views of and attitudes towards marriage. We actually witness the relationships of four different couples through their courtship, engagement and eventual marriage. Through those events and the examples presented to us in the novel of other already married couples, the author engages in a thorough exploration of the theme.

This list is necessarily short. There are whole books devoted to the explanation of literary terms. Some concepts, like style, need to be experienced and discussed in a group setting with plenty of examples in front of you. Others, such as dramatic irony, need keen observation from the student and a close knowledge of the text to appreciate their significance and existence. All such specialist terms are well worth knowing. But they should be used only if they enable you to more effectively express your knowledge and appreciation of the work being studied.